FOLLIES *of* EUROPE
ARCHITECTURAL EXTRAVAGANZAS

Alisin,

thank you for introducing me
to some Cornish extravaganza.

Caroline.

FOLLIES
of EUROPE

ARCHITECTURAL EXTRAVAGANZAS

Photographs by NIC BARLOW

Introduction by TIM KNOX

Text by CAROLINE HOLMES

GARDEN
• ART •
PRESS

CONTENTS

From popes to plutocrats, princes to postmen

This is a book of follies, extravagant edifices raised for the amusement or diversion – and occasionally for the residence – of inspired patrons and artists throughout Europe. Selected by photographer Nic Barlow, these architectural extravaganzas have been assembled not only to demonstrate their charm, diversity and invention, but also to celebrate those that are unexpected, overlooked or little known. From the grandiose conceits that humanise the regal demesnes of Potsdam in Germany (pp. 100–5), to the private cement Elysium created by Mr John Fairnington at Branxton, Northumberland (pp. 214–7), follies owe their existence to an extraordinarily wide range of people. Created by popes and plutocrats, princes and postmen, these buildings stand today as mute testimony to their patrons' taste and discrimination, their passions and peculiarities. While wealth and stability provide the ideal conditions for the birth of architectural curiosities, some have been born out of discord, or commemorate loss and disappointment. Indeed, the stories that these buildings tell are often as evocative as their bizarre forms.

In Europe, it was probably the ancient Romans who first built follies in their gardens and pleasure grounds. Ancient descriptions survive of the villa of Marcus Terentius Varro, a friend of Cicero, at Casinium, midway between Rome and Naples, with its aviaries and arcades. It was destroyed in 47 BC, but the remains of the Egyptian Canopus and other outlandish structures built by the Emperor Hadrian (AD 76–138) at his extensive villa complex at Tivoli outside Rome can still be seen today. Moreover, wall-paintings uncovered in Herculaneum and Pompeii show that the grander Roman gardens were often liberally sprinkled with miniature temples, niches and loggias, ornamented with statues and fountains. The taste for little worlds in miniature survived in the formal gardens of medieval Europe, with their diminutive pasteboard fortresses, bristling with towers and battlements, spiral mounts, and painted and gilded belvederes and arbours. However, almost no trace of these flimsy edifices has survived, apart from in the pages of illuminated manuscripts.

It was the Renaissance popes and the petty princes of the Italian States who revived the practice of garnishing gardens with elaborate architectural conceits in imitation of the ancients. Pirro Ligorio's Casino for Pius IV of *c.*1560, an antiquity-studded aedicule in the Vatican Gardens, was a pioneering building of its kind. The prelates of the Roman Church soon followed suit; the statue-infested terraces, fountains and treacherous *giochi d'acqua* (water jokes) of Cardinal Ippolito II d'Este's eponymous Villa at Tivoli – begun in 1550 and not far from the ruins of the villa of the Emperor Hadrian – was perhaps the most spectacular of them all, full advantage being taken of its precipitous site and the abundant water supply (pp. 28–33). Villa d'Este inspired gardens all over Italy, and even as far afield as Germany and Austria; in 1615, at the archiepiscopal retreat at Hellbrunn, near Salzburg, Archbishop Sittikus

Above: Multi-breasted Fountain of Nature, Villa d'Este, Italy

Page 2: Gazebo, Château de Canon, France

Page 3: One of 600 grotesques, Villa Palagonia, Bagheria, Sicily

Page 4: The mausoleum of the Baron de Castille, Château de Castille, Argilliers, France

imported Italian architects and sculptors to lay out the gardens, and devise ingenious trick fountains (pp. 36–7).

Possibly even more influential were the magnificent palaces and villas of the Medici; notably the villa at Pratolino, to the north of Florence, laid out by Bernardo Buontalenti for Francesco I de'Medici in the 1580s, with its colossal rockwork statue representing the tutelary deity of the place, Appenino, by Giambologna. Most bizarre perhaps was Vicino Orsini's garden of monsters in the Sacro Bosco at Bomarzo, near Viterbo, of 1552–80, although its toothsome grotesques and chimerical buildings disguise a scholarly and highly moralistic itinerary for the educated Renaissance visitor (pp. 22–7).

These famous Italian gardens were admired by travellers and were carefully recorded in engravings. By this means ambitious imitations of Italianate gardens were spawned across Europe, at Fontainebleau in the 1520s for the French king, Francis I, and at Nonsuch Palace, Surrey, England, first for Henry VIII and then for John, Lord Lumley. Created between 1579 and 1591, Lumley's Nonsuch boasted the first grotto and first obelisk in any English garden. Nonsuch Palace has long since been demolished but something of its effect can be conjured up by near-contemporary country house gardens that survive, such as Hardwick Hall in Derbyshire, where extensive outworks in the form of walled courts terminate in domed banqueting houses, ornamented with strapwork and obelisk finials. Even

more elaborate, although actually practical in purpose, was the Triangular Lodge at Rushton in Northamptonshire, built by Catholic politician Sir Thomas Tresham between 1594-6 (pp. 34–5). Ostensibly a residence for the keeper of his rabbit warren, it was also an elaborate architectural act of defiance, loaded with symbolism about his persecuted family and proscribed faith.

The taste for follies was also imported into England by itinerant French architects and engineers, men like Isaac de Caus who, in the early 1630s, filled the gardens of the 4th Earl of Pembroke at Wilton House in Wiltshire with grottoes and ingenious mechanical fountains.

A Spell Cast by Versailles

In France, the successors of Francis I and their Medici-born consorts developed elaborate Italian gardens around the palaces of St Germain and the Luxembourg, but it was at the Palace of Versailles under Louis XIV that a distinctively French style of gardening was developed under the king's gardener and chief architect, André le Nôtre and Jules Hardouin Mansart. With the broad terraces dotted with sculpted vases and statuary, expanses of *parterres de broderie* formed of cut box and coloured gravel, formal fountains and canals, and avenues leading to seemingly endless vistas, the gardens at Versailles formed an impressive setting for the most splendid palace Europe had ever seen. Hidden behind the clipped hedges and towering walls of trellis that

Above, left: Grotto of Neptune, Schloss Hellbrunn, Salzburg, Austria

Above, centre: Grotto in Goldney House, Clifton, Bristol, England

Above, right: Neptune, Sacro Bosco, Bomarzo, Viterbo, Italy

lined the *allées* of this formal framework were a variety
of evocatively named *bosquets* or secret gardens
containing fountains, ornamental buildings, statuary
groups. These included the Bosquet de la Reine, with
its animals and birds of painted lead depicting the fables
of La Fontaine, in settings encrusted with shells and
spars, the Grotte de Thetys, and the Colonnade.

The gardens at Versailles and Marly, a small
neighbouring palace, famed for its waterworks and used
by the king as a private retreat, were to inspire a host of
imitations across Europe. In Italy, Le Nôtre
himself is said to have designed the terraced
gardens at the Villa Torrigiani at Camigliano
for the Lucchese ambassador to France,
Nicolao Santini, although they have been
much altered since (pp. 40–5). At
Herrenhausen, from 1680, the formal gardens
on the model of Versailles were created by the
Electress Sophie, consort of Ernst August,
Elector of Hanover. The attractions at
Herrenhausen include an amphitheatre
bounded by clipped beech hedges and gilded
statuary, and a maze (pp. 46–9). In Holland,
the Stadtholder William and his English wife
Mary laid out the gardens of the Palace of Het
Loo as a sober, Protestant, version of
Versailles, while on their accession to the
throne of England in 1688, Henry VIII's
sprawling old palace of Hampton Court was partially
transformed by Sir Christopher Wren.

The descendants of Louis XIV built palaces inspired
by Versailles; his grandson, Philip V of Spain, laid out
La Granja, near Madrid, between 1720 and 1746,
creating there a watery paradise of fountains, cascades
and canals, all liberally garnished with gilded lead
statuary made by French sculptors (pp. 76–9). La Granja
was the model for the gardens surrounding the Reggia
di Caserta outside Naples, begun in 1751 for Louis XIV's
great-grandson, Charles III, King of the Two Sicilies,
although it was never fully implemented and later
generations softened its formal grandeur (pp. 112–15).

In Austria, the imperial gardens at Schönbrunn in
Vienna were laid out from the 1690s by a succession of
Frenchmen, whose variety of ornamental pavilions in
amusing and evocative architectural styles provided a
welcome retreat from the rigid protocols of court life
conducted within the sprawling palace across the
parterre. This arrangement was modelled on Versailles
and, just as the Emperor of Austria aped the magnificence of the Sun King, so the lesser princes of the
empire imitated Schönbrunn. At Nymphenburg, outside
Munich, the summer palace of the Bavarian rulers,
architect Joseph Effner and French garden designer
Dominique Girard created an extensive formal garden
from 1714, its *bosquets* sheltering a range of miniature
palaces. Just as elaborate were the gardens laid out at
Potsdam from 1715 for Frederick I of Prussia, at first
inspired by the gardens at Marly, and then extended by
his son, Frederick William II, also known as 'Frederick
the Great', whose own palace, Schloss Sanssouci

('without cares'), was a bow-fronted trianon perched upon superimposed terraces fronted by glass-fronted vineries, built between 1744 and 1747 (pp. 100–5). In a glade in the park is the Chinese Tea House, built by J.G. Büring in 1754–7 to accommodate the royal porcelain collection, encircled by a colonnade of gilded palm trees under which sport life-size statues of orientals.

Local topography or traditions often led to surprising variations on the Versailles model. The precipitous site and rugged forests surrounding Schloss Wilhelmshöhe outside Cassel called for an imposing rusticated cascade, topped with a colossal statue of the Farnese Hercules, designed by the Italian Giovanni Francesco Guerniero for Landgrave Karl von Hessen from 1701. The marshy setting of Villa Barbarigo at Valsanzibio, near Padua, created between 1669 and 1702 by the Venetian Senator Antonio Barbarigo, meant that it was best approached by water (pp. 50–3). Thus, visitors entered the garden by boat beneath an imposing watergate, the Portal of Diana, and explored grounds representing the Garden of Eden, teeming with rockwork cascades, *giochi d'acqua*, and even a fortified island garrisoned by a colony of rabbits. In Portugal, the Italianate gardens surrounding the Palácio da Fronteira outside Lisbon, created for Dom João de Mascarenhas, Marquis of Fronteira, from 1670, are extended by illusionist vistas depicting fantastic gardens painted on the local tiles or *azulejos* (pp. 54–7). But nobody wanted to copy the decadent excesses of the Villa Palagonia, built for the eccentric, half-mad Prince Francesco Ferdinando

Palagonia Gravina at the resort of Bagheria, outside Palermo, from 1715. Only a few statues of monsters and dwarfs survive today from the grotesque guard of honour that once surmounted its strange corridor-like walled entrance avenue, but the palace still retains some of its wild décor of distorting mirrors and swirling marbling (pp. 70–5).

Follies and the English Landscape

Nowhere did follies catch on more than in England, where long periods of peace and political stability under the Hanoverians, and the growing wealth and power of the landed classes, encouraged the building of increasingly ambitious country houses. Scarcely less important were their parks and gardens, for in Britain – where land ownership has traditionally been all important – the aristocracy and gentry spent a considerable amount of time on their estates, lavishing fortunes on buildings and gardens, rather than maintaining an expensive establishment at Court. The results of this investment can be seen in the engraved views of country seats by Johannes Knip and Leonard Knyff in *Britannia Illustrata* (1707), bird's-eye views showing houses set amidst elaborate gardens and dependencies, their parks criss-crossed with radiating avenues. Ornamental garden

Above, left: The Garden of Venus, Villa Torrigiani, Lucca, Italy
Above, right: The Monsters, Villa Palagonia, Italy
Below: The Portal of Diana, Villa Barbarigo Pizzoni Ardemani, Valsanzibio, Italy

buildings such as banqueting houses, pavilions,
belvederes, and seats in a variety of evocative
architectural styles were *de rigueur*.

Castle Howard, laid out by Sir John Vanbrugh and
Nicholas Hawksmoor for the 3rd Earl of Carlisle from
1715, boasted a rotunda, a triumphal arch and a vast
domed mausoleum. Horace Walpole wrote of it after a
visit in 1772: 'Nobody … had informed me that I
should at one view see a palace, a town, a fortified city,
temples on high places, woods worthy of being each a
metropolis of the Druids, vales connected to hills by
other woods, the noblest lawn in the world fenced by
half a horizon, and a mausoleum that would tempt one
to be buried alive.' At Stowe in Buckinghamshire, the
bewildering number of garden structures provoked
censure from foreign commentators. On the margins of
the formal gardens created for Sir Richard Temple,
later Viscount Cobham, and laid out by Charles
Bridgeman from 1715, some of the earliest experiments
in irregular gardening were carried out and, after
Cobham's disgrace in 1733, the architect and painter
William Kent devised the Elysian Fields, a secret valley
dotted with classical structures freighted with a bitter
political message, and overlooking a stream – the
Worthies River (pp. 64–9). Few other country house
proprietors had the resources, or the inclination, to
copy Cobham's rancorous 'garden of exile', but Kent's
painterly combination of artfully naturalised 'Arcadian'
landscape and picturesque buildings was to have many

imitators and led to the development of an indigenous
garden style – the English landscape garden – which is
arguably Britain's most important artistic innovation.

The inspiration of the English landscape garden
was not purely classical. The celebrated water gardens
at Studley Royal, near Ripon in Yorkshire, created
from 1716, culminated in the imposing, moss-grown
ruins of a thirteenth-century Cistercian monastery. At
Stourhead, Wiltshire, begun by banker Henry Hoare II
in 1740, miniature copies of the Roman Pantheon and
the Temple of the Sun at Palmyra vie for attention with
a rustic hermitage, a genuine medieval market cross
(brought here from the centre of Bristol) and, high up
in the woods, a Gothic nunnery (pp. 90–5).

Despite their extravagant and essentially frivolous
character, the buildings, statues and learned inscriptions
in English landscape gardens often formed part of a
highly allusive tour, littered with references to classical
mythology, literature, morals and even contemporary
politics. Most of the grandest gardens were open to the
public, although tips or 'vails' had to be paid to the
servants who showed you round. Some boasted guide-
books, spas, and even hotels at the lodge gates. Such was
the British mania for ornamental garden buildings that
even purely utilitarian structures assumed fanciful dress;
a greenhouse for growing pineapples at Dunmore, near
Stirling, is topped by an 11m/37ft high stone replica of
the prickly fruit, which was then both highly prized and
notoriously difficult to grow (pp. 118–19). Less obviously

useful is the clutch of strange edifices, erected between 1803 and 1834, which enlivened John Fuller's estate at Brightling, Sussex. These included a rotunda temple, an observatory, and various obelisks and pillars, one of which, the Sugar Loaf, is a replica of a neighbouring church spire and was built to satisfy a wager. 'Mad Jack' Fuller also built a pyramidal mausoleum for himself in Brightling churchyard, in which, it was rumoured, he was interred, fully dressed, sitting at table with a fowl and a bottle of port (pp. 134–5). Still more useless are the rubble follies in Barwick Park, near Yeovil, Somerset, said to have been built by the Messiter family to relieve unemployment in the 1820s (pp. 144–5). Towering, sinister and seemingly without a practical purpose, they rejoice in equally puzzling names – the Cone, the Fish Tower and Jack the Treacle-Eater.

Eccentricities and Escapism

An even more pronounced streak of eccentricity can be detected in the follies built in Ireland by Anglo-Irish landowners. Capricious and wayward like their creators, the demesnes of great Irish houses spring surprises like the Folly at Castletown, Co. Kildare, a 42m/140ft high copulation between a triumphal arch and an obelisk, built in 1740 by Mrs Katherine Conolly both as a monument to her late husband, the famous Speaker Conolly, and to give employment during a hard winter. Another of Mrs Conolly's famine relief schemes, this time of 1743, is the Wonder Barn, a conical granary

encircled by a staircase. In Belvedere Park, Co. Westmeath, is the Jealous Wall, a 55m/180ft long stretch of remarkably convincing ruined castle wall, the largest sham ruin in Ireland. It was erected around 1760 by Robert Rochfort, 1st Earl of Belvedere, to shut out the view of a neighbouring house built by his estranged brother (pp. 116–17). In the charming Ferme Ornée at Larchill, Co. Kildare, the grounds were dotted with strange primitive Gothic farm buildings, together with a fort on the lake called Gibraltar, and structures called the Foxes' Earth and the Eel House (pp. 106–11). Scarcely less expected is the domed Mussenden Temple at Downhill, Co. Derry, built in the 1700s, an evocation of the Temple of Vesta at Tivoli perched on a rocky cliff overlooking Magilligan Strand and the Giant's Causeway (pp. 126–7). Here Frederick Augustus Hervey, Bishop of Derry and 4th Earl of Bristol, could read Lucretius in the comfort of a luxuriously fitted-out library, high above the roaring Atlantic Ocean.

Thanks to engravings, pattern books and visitors' descriptions, the English landscape style gradually gained favour in France where the fashion for what were termed *jardins anglo-chinois* led to the destruction of many of the *bosquets* at Versailles. At the Petit Trianon, Madame de Pompadour's instructive botanic garden was superseded by a picturesque garden on English lines, laid out by Richard Mique for Marie-Antoinette from 1774. With its Temple of Love, rockwork grotto, and hamlet of rustic farm buildings, the gardens at the

Above, left: Gothic Temple, Bramham Park, Wetherby, England
Above, centre: Worcester Lodge, Badminton, England
Above, right: Belvedere House, Belvedere House, Mullingar, Ireland

Petit Trianon became a byword for luxurious escapism. A similar transformation was wrought on the gardens of the Château de Rambouillet, near Yvelines, where the Duc de Penthièvre swept away a garden by Le Nôtre in 1779 and laid out a *jardin anglais* with winding walks and shrubberies, dotted with ornamental *fabriques*. Louis XVI bought it for Marie-Antoinette in 1783 and it was here that she built her infamous Dairy, a dainty marmoreal fantasy equipped with Sèvres porcelain milk pails, where she could play at being a rustic. The king's brother, the Comte d'Artois, commissioned the Scottish gardener Alexander Blaikie to lay out similarly

Above: Gibraltar, Larchill, Co. Kildare, Ireland

informal gardens at the Château de Bagatelle in the Bois de Boulogne outside Paris. Completed by 1786, the glades were enlivened by structures in the Egyptian, Chinese, Dutch and Indian style.

Exotic buildings had long been popular in French gardens – the Duc de Choiseul had built the seven-storey tiered Pagoda at Chanteloup between 1773 and 1778 (pp. 124–5), a 'temple of fidelity' to those friends who remained faithful to him after his disgrace from court in 1770 – but follies proliferated in the gardens of the *maisons de plaisir* created by nobles and tax farmers on the eve of the Revolution, places like Parc Monceau, Méréville, and L'Isle Adam. At the Désert de Retz, deep in the forest of Marly, between 1774 and 1789 François Nicholas Henri Racine de Monville created an enchanted glade with a Chinese house, a Tartar tent and a pyramid, while even the house itself was in the form of a huge truncated column (pp. 121–3).

Expensive and impractical, many of these French gardens perished, like their owners, during the French Revolution; Parc Monceau and the Bagatelle are now municipal Parisian parks, and most of the monuments of Méréville have been moved to the nearby Parc de Jeurre. But at Wörlitz, near Dessau in north-east Germany, elaborate gardens laid out during the 1790s by Leopold III, Prince of Anhalt-Dessau, survive. The multitude of evocative structures at Wörlitz mirrors the cosmopolitan interests of the prince and the buildings he had admired during his extensive travels in Europe, even exceeding Stowe in their number and variety. Still more extensive was the palace-strewn landscape created for the Prussian royal family at Potsdam by the architect G.F. Schinkel and the landscape gardener Peter Joseph Lenné, uniting the various palaces and parks on the banks of the River Havel, among them Charlottenhof, Schinkel's exquisite Italianate villa for Crown Prince Frederick William of 1826, incorporating a miniature Roman Baths complex.

In Italy the informal English landscape style was imported by the French and led to the 'naturalisation' of many of the famous formal gardens, which in any case were ruinously expensive to maintain. Conservative Catholic Spain was less entranced by English gardens, a rare example being those of El Capricio de la Alameda, at Osuna, near Madrid, laid out in the late eighteenth century by the Anglophile Duchess of Osuna, a progressive and patroness of Goya.

The Battle of Styles

The mania for bizarre buildings did not abate in the nineteenth century. Between 1787 and 1823, the sovereign himself, the Prince Regent, later King George IV of England, transformed his marine residence on the Sussex coast into an onion-domed Asiatic palace, lavishly decorated in the Chinese taste within (pp. 136–41). Miraculously, the Royal Pavilion in Brighton survives intact with many of its fittings and furnishings, although Humphry Repton's design of 1808 for embellishing its pleasure grounds with a parrot house inspired by the temple at Bindrabund,

India, was never carried out. Meanwhile in Exmouth, Devon, in 1798 the Misses Jane and Mary Parminter, spinster cousins just returned from a Grand Tour, set about building a house inspired by the church of San Vitale at Ravenna. Christened 'A La Ronde', the interior of the sixteen-sided *cottage orné* was decorated by the ladies with shells, seeds, minerals, curled paper and feathers.

Many proprietors made a speciality of a particular style in their gardens; a retired East India nabob erected 'Hindoo' buildings in the grounds at Sezincote, Gloucestershire, while feudal Gothic was thought more appropriate at ducal Lismore Castle, Co. Waterford. Millionaire William Waldorf Astor installed his Roman Grand Tour booty on the terraces at Cliveden, Buckinghamshire, although no one knows why Lady Broughton built a clever facsimile of the Mer de Glace in her rockery at Hoole House, Cheshire. Visitors to the grounds of Biddulph Grange, Staffordshire, wandered through gardens called 'China' and 'Egypt', complete with a section of the Great Wall, a joss house and a pylon formed of clipped yew, flanked by sphinxes, but the inspiration behind the mysterious Cretan labyrinth of paths and follies around the lake at Stancombe Park, Gloucestershire, remains obscure (pp. 142–3). Combining Egyptian and Moorish features, and a whalebone arch, it is generally attributed to the mid-nineteenth-century owner of the house, the Reverend David Edwards, who is said to have used the

delicate Tuscan lakeside summerhouse for romantic assignations with his gypsy mistress.

Over the course of the nineteenth century the battle of styles also raged across Europe. Nowhere can the stylistic schizophrenia of the era be seen in such luxurious profusion than at Sintra, outside Lisbon, where the mild climate, dramatic topography and tolerant neighbours encouraged wild excesses. An early settler was William Beckford, later famous as the 'Caliph of Fonthill', who lived here in the 1790s. His diminutive Gothic house, the Quinta de Monserrate, was later rebuilt as the astonishing Moorish-Gothic villa of the Englishman Sir Francis Cook, 'visconde de Monserrate', who bought the estate in 1865 and restocked Beckford's gardens with many rare and exotic plants (pp. 162–3). Nearby is another scenographic fantasy, the Quinta da Regaleira, created for Dr Antonio Carvalho Montiero, a cultivated bibliophile with a fortune derived from Brazilian coffee and precious stones. Between 1898 and 1910, the Italian architect and theatre designer Luigi Manini, conjured up for him not only a substantial country house, fiercely crocketed and traceried in the neo-Manueline style, but also a host of distinctly unnerving garden features, all with a mystic Rosicrucian theme (pp. 174–7). But perhaps the most imposing is the Palácio da Pena, perched high on the peak of the Serra de Sintra, rebuilt by Dom Fernando II, King Consort of Queen Maria II of Portugal, on the site of an ancient monastery. Dom Fernando's architect

Above, left: Column House, Désert de Retz, France
Above, centre: Minerva in the Maze, Villa Nazionale Pisani, Stra, Italy
Above, right: The Gothic House, Wörlitz, Germany

Above, left: The Chinese Tea Houses, Stancombe Park, England

Above, centre: The Palace, Quinta de Monserrate, Portugal

Above, right: The Chinese Bridge, Temple and Tea Terrace, Biddulph Grange, England

Below: The Moorish Kiosk, Schloss Linderhof, Germany

was Baron Wilhelm Ludwig von Eshwege, who constructed here, from the 1830s, the enchanting red and yellow washed fairy fortress, once compared by Richard Strauss to the 'Castle of the Holy Grail' (pp. 150–3). Dom Fernando was born a German prince, of the House of Saxe-Coburg-Gotha, so it is no wonder that this is a fantasy castle on a par with Neuschwanstein, the turreted Wagnerian confection built by his kinsman, the 'mad' King Ludwig II of Bavaria 1869–1884. At Schloss Linderhof, near Garmisch-Partenkirchen, Upper Bavaria, built between 1868 and 1880, King Ludwig created a miniature Versailles with formal and informal gardens teeming with ornamental buildings, among them a mosque covered in painted tiles, and a banded Moorish kiosk (*see* p. 167).

Visionaries and Dreamers

Ludwig II and Dom Fernando required vast fortunes to realise their expensive visions, but there is also a strong tradition of very ordinary people building follies from simple and inexpensive materials that are no less impressive or inventive, particularly in the late nineteenth and early twentieth centuries, when – for a time at least – novelty of follies seems to have palled for the very rich. Thus the mysterious subterranean grotto at Margate, located beneath a terrace of ordinary houses in this down-at-heel seaside resort in Kent, is Cockney heir to the tradition of aristocratic grottoes found in many eighteenth-century parks.

France has a seemingly inexhaustible supply of petit-bourgeois follies, many of them deploying that French artisan speciality, realistic rocks and twigs made from cement. The possibilities of cement were pushed to the limits at Le Palais Idéal of Le Facteur Cheval, a bizarre Angkor Wat-like edifice built in the back garden of a house in the village of Hauterives, near Lyons. Constructed entirely with his own hands by Ferdinand Cheval, the village postman, it was begun in 1879 and only finished in 1912. With its squat 'Assyrian' columns, preposterous long-legged atlantes representing Caesar, Vercingétorix and Archimedes, and cryptic inscriptions, it is little wonder that it became a favourite of the Surrealists (pp. 168–73). Monsieur Cheval died in 1924, but not before creating a mausoleum for himself in the local graveyard, its exterior a mass of writhing, vermicelli-like cement. Shards of broken crockery cover the exterior and interior of La Maison Picassiette in a side street in Chartres, created by manual worker Raymond Isidore between 1938 and 1964 as a house for himself and his long-suffering family (pp. 194–7). All the furniture, including the beds, are coated with crockery, an 'outsider' version of the sophisticated ceramic *bricolage* employed in 1900 by the great Catalan architect, Antoni Gaudí, to cheer up Parc Güell in Barcelona (pp. 184–7).

Even in the turbulent later years of the twentieth century there were still visionaries and dreamers who sought to escape from the world by creating their own Elysia. At the Château de Groussay, Montfort l'Aumary, France, the immensely wealthy aesthete Charles de Beistegui evoked a perfect eighteenth-century landscape garden between 1952 and 1970 with help from Emilio

Terry and Alexandre Serebriakoff (pp. 198–203). Groussay has a pyramid, Palladian bridge, Chinese pagoda and observatory column – many of them exquisite variants on eighteenth-century buildings Beistegui had admired in England, France, Sweden and even Russia.

Meanwhile at La Scarzuola, near to Orvieto, from 1958, the Milanese architect Tomaso Buzzi designed and built an 'Ideal City' of Mannerist towers and temples next to the ancient Franciscan convent where he lived until his death in 1981 (pp. 206–13). Inspired by Francesco Colonna's enigmatic *Hypnerotomachia Poliphili* (1499), and Hadrian's Villa at Tivoli, Buzzi's strange 'Città Buzziana' is a stylised capriccio of buildings he admired, arranged in seven open-air theatres, like a petrified stage set by Giovanni Battista Piranesi and Giorgio de Chirico.

In Britain there is Portmeirion, at Penrhyndeudraeth on the coast of north Wales, a beguiling toy-town of architectural salvage conceived by architect Sir Clough Williams-Ellis both as a business venture and as 'a home for fallen buildings' (pp. 188–93). Established as a speculative enterprise in 1941 and continually added to by Williams-Ellis until his death in 1972, Portmeirion has long been a favourite tourist resort and film location.

Tourism and publicity is the powerful impetus behind the creation of the Parco di Pinocchio, at Collodi, a tourist attraction dating from 1953, with its kitsch mosaics and metal sculptures (pp. 204–5), while the manufacturers of Swarovski Crystal are still developing the Swarovski Kristallwelten at Innsbruck, Austria, a crystalline wonderland designed by André Heller, complete with a monstrous mossy fountainhead (with blazing Swarovski Crystal eyes) and a maze in the form of a human hand (pp. 236–7). Austria is not usually known for bold eccentricity, but it abounds at the zany Hundertwasser Spa at Bad Blumau, near Graz in south-east Styria, designed by Friedensreich Hundertwasser, self-styled 'doctor for sick architecture'. Built in 1995–7, it claims to be the 'world's largest habitable work of art', and sports uneven floors, 'joyous' primary-coloured walls and columns, and grass-covered roofs (pp. 230–5).

Follies and similar extravaganzas are still very much being built today in the twenty-first century, as can be seen in the photographs of a Russian dacha only erected in 2002 which, with its distinctive onion domes and wooden bargeboards, surprises walkers in a damp Shropshire valley near Ludlow (pp. 226–9), or the ancient-looking drystone folly of Sheep's Barn, Wiltshire, which is only a few years old (pp. 222–5). Nor are all modern follies evocative or dependent on older styles of architecture. I.M. Pei's pagoda-like steel and glass pavilion, erected in millennium year in the grounds of Oare House, near Marlborough, Wiltshire (pp. 242–3), demonstrates how, with its proud confidence and enhanced technical capabilities, tomorrow's architecture is well suited to the buildings of caprice.

Tim Knox
London, 2008

Above, left: Castellated gate, La Maison Picassiette, Chartres, France
Above, centre: Le Palais Idéal, Hauterives, France
Above, right: Parc Güell, Barcelona, Spain

ALLEGORY & FANTASY

Power, order and conceit form the bedrock of the allegorical and fantastical gardens of the sixteenth and seventeenth centuries. Art is superior to nature and a patron's power and virtue are overtly celebrated in the theatrical design of his demesne. This philosophy was fulfilled with brio by cultured minds well versed in mathematics, cosmology and music – intellectual gymnastics for the cognoscenti.

The architecture of the Renaissance garden evolved into the Mannerist showcase for collections of antique sculpture juxtaposed with architectural flights of fantasy that could be read for allegorical and moral instruction. The harmony and order associated with Apollo, sun god and the god of architecture, were matched by feats of hydraulic engineering that harnessed the might of Poseidon, the river god, to spectacular effect. Follies take no account of labour but, ironically, Hercules is ever present.

Château de la Bastie d'Urfé, Saint-Étienne-le-Molard

At the Château de la Bastie (de la Bâtie in its modern form), tucked away in the isolated Forez region near Lyons, is a gloriously extravagant shell-encrusted *salle de fraîcheur* linked to a chapel. Symbolic of sensual pleasure preceding spiritual refreshment and the allegorical journey from the pagan to the Christian world, in 1548 it was unknown in France for a grotto to lead to a chapel, and this is reputedly the sole surviving example of its kind in the country.

Equally, the grotto is an evocation of the Renaissance notion that raw nature should be refashioned and polished by the power of man for the glory of God. Its creator, Claude d'Urfé, served as a courtier to two French kings – Francis I and Henry II – and acted as French Ambassador at the Council of Trent in Italy, and the grotto has marked similarities with the one at the Bishop's Palace in Trento and the contemporary engravings of Agostino Veneziano.

Above: Neptune listening to the ocean

Opposite: Pan flanked by shell-work figures in the Salle de Fraîcheur

The Italian grotto, created within hilly terraces and associated with entry into the depths of the earth, required reinterpretation when translated to flatter French terrain – either a place had to be found in the château itself or, if it was to be sited in the garden, a building had to be constructed to shelter it. Far from detracting from its symbolic value, a grotto placed next to a chapel allowed the residents to contemplate their darker, inner selves before passing into the light of regular worship.

The grotto in the Château de la Bastie is large (about 10.5 by 5.5m/35 by 18ft and 3.5m/11ft high), with five bays on the north wall which correspond to arcading on the south wall in the form of three niches and two *alveoli* or cell-like apses with elaborate shell-work, vaulting above and geometric motifs below. The vaulting is coffered in imitation of Hadrian's Pantheon in Rome – an architectural ornamental device that resonates through Palladian and Italianate designs into the twentieth century. The ornamentation is realised in *sable collé* or coloured sands glued to wooden ceilings in geometric motifs and the floors feature pebbled mosaics. The floor is divided into eight compartments, the partitions marked out in shells, and the two largest areas signal the entrance to the chapel. The remaining sides have panels and doors that disguise the asymmetry of the room, and all are decorated with rich swags of shells. It is likely that the workmen were trained by artists from the École de Fontainebleau where an internal grotto was also created.

In the crepuscular darkness, arched treillage ornamented with golden vine branches adds to the dreamlike atmosphere of the grotto, since D'Urfé, like Orsini at Bomarzo (pp. 22–7), would have been familiar with the monk Francesco Colonna's *Hypnerotomachia Poliphili* or *Dream of Poliphilus* of 1467 which was published in Venice in 1499. Illustrated with innovative woodcuts of fantastic Renaissance landscapes that included sculpture, waterworks, perspective and topiary, Colonna's narrative journey is a Humanist quest for spiritual truth woven into a romance. Its roots

lie in the realms of fable and medieval Arthurian romances set in an enchanted but deceitful garden. Full of snares for the unwary, its victim could be tempted by illusions and thus fall prey to vice. In his search for truth, the hero Poliphilus undergoes a series of initiations, which, if successful, lead him to the goal of glory or love. The tradition of the enchanted garden, in which love – profane or sacred – is seen as something to be pursued by way of all kinds of unforeseen obstacles, was developed in the stories of Ludovico Ariosto, Torquato Tasso and, in the seventeenth century, was explored by Claude d'Urfé's descendant Honoré in the pastoral romance *L'Astrée*.

At her death in 1621, Claude's granddaughter Anne d'Urfé left a detailed description of the garden at the Château de la Bastie. She included a brief outline of the grotto and chapel, dating its creation to 1548, and wrote of marble statues brought from Italy – the most beautiful in the realm in her estimation! Among huge statues of the four seasons, 'Autumn' was nine feet (2.7m) tall. The rest of the grotto was 'marvellous', according to Anne d'Urfé, as a result of the industrious application of small stones enlivened by many tiny jets of water.

The lead plumbing still works but 'Autumn' is long gone. Pan remains (*left*), flanked by shell-work figures – possibly Vertumnus and Pomona or just a satyr and maenad. As Pan was in the cortege of Bacchus, the latter might have been part of the great 'Autumn' at the entrance. 'Winter', said to be a portrait of Claude d'Urfé, is grey haired and swathed in a cloak against a chevroned background – seemingly all passion spent. A panel depicts a fish-tailed Neptune (p. 18) with his ear to a shell listening to the sea. He carries a triton and there are birds flying over with shells wrought into clouds.

Created far away from the French centres of power, this extraordinary sixteenth-century allegorical survival provides a fantastic insight into the Renaissance mind.

Opposite, above and detail of the Salle de Fraîcheur

Sacro Bosco, Bomarzo

Are follies lunacy or a joyful exercise in sanity? Fifteen years before he retired as a soldier in Pope Paul III's army, Pier Francesco Vicino Orsini planted a *sacro bosco* (sacred grove) on a rocky rugged site away from his villa near Viterbo, the capital of the province of Lazio. From 1567 this woodland landscape on three levels became the setting for Orsini's exploration of man's journey through the snares and passions of life to the ultimate goal of understanding divine love.

Orsini, an important figure in the intellectual circles of Rome and the Vatican, was a thoughtful observer of man's folly in battle, politics and love. Pirro Ligorio acted as his amanuensis, as he did for Cardinal d'Este (pp. 28–33). Like Claude d'Urfé, Orsini and Ligorio would have undoubtedly read the *Hypnerotomachia Poliphili* or *Dream of Poliphilus*, which follows Poliphilus' journey in his quest for truth with his beloved Polia.

The sphinxes of Greek mythology guard the entrance to the Sacro Bosco with a warning: 'Who walks in this garden without raising their eyebrows and remains tight-lipped will never admire the seven wonders of the world.' Orsini may have used Turkish prisoners of war to carve the rock into the cast of players that act out the numerous allegorical and fantastical scenes, including the gaping mouth of Glaucus (p. 24) who,

Above: Neptune
Opposite: Prince Astolfo mounted on an elephant

according to mythology, after eating the horned poppy, *Glaucium*, was turned into a sea god.

In the rock-hewn figures, many allusions to the antique are obscure, but references to scenes in the poet Ludovico Ariosto's romantic epic *Orlando Furioso* are much easier to interpret. It was Ariosto's writings that established the literary form of *commedia erudita* (learned comedy). Gripped by madness, Orlando, the size of a colossus, furiously tears apart the body of an innocent woodcutter, his arms powerful and yet his face verging on the disinterested. Sanity literally pours from the hand of Prince Astolfo (*opposite*), mounted on an elephant, into the nostrils of Orlando, furious in his madness but controlled by the firm grasp of the elephant's trunk. The elephant represents Hannibal's great march across the Alps and is, therefore, a symbol of strength.

In the sixteenth century, water articulated Orsini's narrative. Neptune (*left*) holds a small dolphin in his right hand that represents the River Tiber, an allegory of controlling waters – sea or river – that runs timelessly through landscape history. A torrent gushes past a turtle plodding towards the open mouth of a sea monster, its domed shell supporting a statue of Fame blowing a trumpet. The message is simple: 'Festina lente' – 'Make haste slowly.' Beyond there is a statue of Pegasus, the winged horse that galloped between the Muses and creativity, an allegory much used by pretentious contemporaries. However, Orsini wished subtly to fly in the face of convention by straight-forward language and liberal thinking but not to the

extent of attracting the attentions of the Italian Inquisition. So is Pegasus actually flying into the scheme or away from the folly of pomposity?

Just as Dante's *Inferno* encompassed concentric circles that descended into a pit entered from the middle of a dark wood, at Bomarzo steps lead up into the screaming Mouth of Hell (*left*), the well of evil darkness that threatens destiny. This vision of horror – staring eyes, flaring nostrils, baring teeth – has fleshy lips carved with Dante's words 'Lasciate ogne speranza, voi ch'intrate' – 'Abandon hope all ye who enter here.' Speak in this mouth with care, for the voice is amplified and distorted so as to be heard throughout the Sacro Bosco. However, within this fantasy hell is hospitality, a large tongue doubling as a table, ideal for picnics; at night, lamps were placed in the eyes.

After the dank darkness of the valley you climb to a plateau lined with urns known as the Moonscape. Urns traditionally contained the ashes of the dead, and the largest holds those of Orlando; here the allegory goes further, for both Ariosto and Dante believed the moon

Above: The Turtle with Fame blowing a trumpet with the Sea Monster on the left
Left: The Mouth of Hell
Opposite: The gaping mouth of Glaucus

Above: The Leaning House
by the Moonscape
Opposite: Hercules kills
Cacus by quartering him
with his bare hands

to be a place where the wits of lost souls were bottled up. At one end the crazily proportioned Crooked or Leaning House, albeit well built, is an architect's nightmare but with harmony and order restored inside. The grotesque laughing 'Mask of Madness' was cut from the living rock and topped with the globe and castle that formed Orsini's crest.

There is a mossy maturity to this landscape, Orsini taking you through time from the primeval mists of antiquity and the Great Flood to Italy's earliest Etruscan civilisation, represented by a ruined temple. At the highest level stands the 'Temple in the Meadow', an exquisitely built monument dedicated to the love of his life, Julia Farnese Orsini, who had died young. The temple portico leads into a domed chapel – a potent symbol of salvation from terrible forces and the pleasures of a rational world.

After Orsini's death in 1584, the paradox of Bomarzo was fulfilled as the sculptures were reclaimed by nature. In the 1940s the Italian art critic and collector Mario Praz brought Salvador Dalí to explore these fragmented narratives. Famed for his Surrealist paintings Dalí worked on numerous film projects, testing and exploring his distinctive imagery and ideas, not least of which was the dream sequence in Alfred Hitchcock's 1945 film *Spellbound*. Just as *sacro* means both holy and magical, so ambiguity informed the film made by Praz and Dalí.

Bomarzo's folly-filled landscape of allegory and fantasy, which even in the sixteenth century flew in the face of convention, remains inspirational, influencing among others Jean Cocteau, Niki de St Phalle (the Tarot Garden at Garavicchio-Capalbio, Tuscany) and Alberto Ginastera, who entitled his 1967 opera *Bomarzo*.

Villa d'Este, Tivoli

From Villa d'Este, Cardinal Ippolito d'Este could contemplate the shining dome of St Peter's in Rome, some 40km/25 miles to the west, whilst relishing the respite of Tivoli's balmy climate. D'Este had tried and failed three times to become pope; however, as

Governor of Tivoli, he could channel his thwarted ambition and the waters of the town into the creation of a personal paradise.

Through the fantasy of the garden the cardinal forged a link with imperial Rome, the allegory masterminded by Pirro Ligorio on the vertiginous slopes of a former convent. During the 1550s Ligorio was excavating the nearby Roman site of the Emperor Hadrian's Villa (Villa Adriana) from which he could plunder suitable imperial statues and marbles. Tivoli and

Above: The Fountain of the Dragons *(detail)*
Opposite: The nurturing breasts of Mother Nature sculpted by Gillis van den Vliete inspired by the classical Diana of Ephesus
Overleaf: Nearly 300 jets line the Alley of a Hundred Fountains

its elevated environs attracted other cardinals who also created summer homes, so the politicking of Rome coninued unabated.

In the sixteenth century you entered the grounds through a gate from the town, up a steep path and under a pergola, an exercise in tunnel vision so that as the pergola ended the vastness of the scheme surprised you. How far Cardinal d'Este travelled down the garden to greet you indicated your importance. You had become part of a sophisticated allegorical parlour game played on many levels – physical and intellectual. The cardinal-

creator could look down personally or in the form of flattering associated effigies such as Hercules, whose labours on the hard, steep route to virtue were popular allegories throughout Europe, represented in suitably Herculean monuments.

Early in the ascent of the gardens the route divides at the Fountain of the Dragons (detail, *left*), one of the four winged dragons that are emblematic of the pope. Which path to take? The gently rising walk to pleasurable vice in the Grotto of Venus or the steep climb to virtue and the Grotto of Diana? Mother's milk is the most virtuous fluid and it flows in abundance from the multi-breasted Fountain of Nature (*right*), inspired by the classical portrayal of Diana of Ephesus. En route are many shady corners offering privacy for gossip, trysts or simply reading aloud.

Power over water, gushing, splashing, murmuring, silent – spectacular effects from jokes to musical organs – equates with power over life. Ligorio (with Orazio Olivieri, the hydraulics engineer and the roman architect Giacomo della Posta) was inspired by the classical architectural writer Vitruvius, who had devoted one of his ten books on architecture to water. Nearly three hundred jets line the Alley of a Hundred Fountains (*overleaf*) from whose misty, mossy depths Ovid's classical characters metamorphose into animal form. Originally water on the lowest layer shot out of a menagerie of beasts' mouths, each a different relief of Ovid's characters who had taken the form of a dog, deer, bear, bat, and so on. A cocktail of classical and Christian allegory, as well as classical figures, nature transformed

Above: The Fountains of Rome, The genesis of Rometta or Little Rome: the river god Aniene shelters under the Tiburtine Mountain
Opposite: Detail of the Fountain of the Organ, with Apollo to the left and Orpheus beyond to the right

as the green blade of spring rose after winter, a visual parallel with the transfiguration of Christ.

The Oval Fountain, now known as the Tivoli Fountain, is fed from an overflowing basin under which a colossal statue of the Tiburtine Sybil and her son Melicerte shelter. They are flanked by reclining river gods and ten Nereids in an artificial ferny landscape; this is punctuated with jets and fans of fine misty water and a balustrade with urns trailing tiny spouts of water. Water stills into mirrors, then actively encapsulates the Holy City in the watery landscape of Rometta (*above*), planned by Ligorio and realised by Curzio Maccarone. The genesis of Rometta or Little Rome is the river god Aniene who shelters under the Tiburtine Mountain holding the Temple of the Sibyl, while the godly Appenines cradle the embryonic Tiber. It is set around seven miniature hills sheltering replicas of the temples and palaces of Rome. One statue of the 'Lion tearing

the Horse' is an allegory of Tivoli's subjugation to Rome, a fantasy used two hundred years later by William Kent in the allegorical landscape he created for General Dormer at Rousham in England.

One of the hydraulic masterpieces was the music played by the Fountain of the Organ (detail, *opposite*), designed by Tommaso Ghinucci, and the pipes still play jets up to 12m/40ft into the air accompanied by replica music. How appropriate that it is decorated with Apollo with his lyre while, beyond, Orpheus plays to tame the animals and break rock into soil. Leave the piped music and listen out for the twittering of bronze birds as the water pressure builds up in the Owl Fountain. When the pressure becomes too much the owl turns to silence them, and in the hush the cuckoo responds.

Today you start the journey at the villa, so like Cardinal d'Este you can decide just how far down the incline you want to go.

Rushton Triangular Lodge, Kettering

1593 dates the building, triangle and trefoil of the three-in-one and one-in-three that are fantastically portrayed in the Triangular Lodge at Rushton, north-west of Kettering in Northamptonshire. The Holy Trinity plays as important a part in the faith of the Church of Rome as that of England, so a devout Elizabethan man could safely use it as the central motif on his triangular lodge. Thomas Tresham embodied the ideal Renaissance man who liked to exercise his intellectual prowess, especially in mathematics and, possibly, in black magic. His estate was extensive and, amongst his riches, was a fabulous library with at least seven books on the then popular subject of emblems and their meanings. Although a loyal subject, his conversion to Catholicism in 1580 resulted in many years of imprisonment, fines and forfeits.

Ostensibly the magnificent Triangular Lodge was built to house Tresham's warrener with ample cellarage for body storage, rabbit warrens being an important adjunct to great estates, providing winter meat and fur. Decoratively rabbits symbolised fecundity, and were also an allegory of vulnerability in the hands of their master.

However, constructed on the basis of an equilateral triangle, the lodge has many layers of meaning to demonstrate Tresham's faith. There is an angelic host under the roof with the covert letters SSSDDS and QEEQEEQVE that relate to the treasonable prayers within the Catholic Mass – *Sanctus, Sanctus, Sanctus Dominus Deus Sabbath* and *Qui Erat et Qui Est et Qui Venturus Est*. Reading the three walls on four levels and

continuing to the topmost pinnacle is an exercise in multiple devices of three. Approached across the estate, the lodge stood alone in grass. Above the narrow door are '5555' and 'Tres testimonium dant' – a play on Tresham's name and the number three. 55 is a code used to represent Jesus Maria, and the upper storey is 33ft feet wide, the age at which Jesus Christ was crucified.

On each side of the building runs a text thirty-three letters long, which on the north side reads, 'Quis separabit nos a charitate Christi' (Who shall separate us from the love of Christ). On this same side 1595 dates the completion of the building and 1641 is said to be an exercise in numerology associated with the cult of the Virgin Mary (1641 minus 1593 equals 48, the year of the death of the Virgin), which was banned in the Church of England and supplanted by that of Elizabeth. To Tresham the dove caring for her chicks represents both God's care for his children and that of the Virgin Mary.

Mottoes in three parts include: 'Mentes tuorum visita' (Visit the minds of thy people), and 'Respicite non mihi soli laboravi' (Look, I have not worked only for myself). Above ECCE, the lamb triumphant (not the sacrificial lamb) holds the flag of victory – the origin of pubs called 'The Lamb and Flag'.

This triangular religious gem has become an allegory for the folly of Tresham's faith, while much of its message remains a mystery.

Above: 1593 dates the building, triangle and trefoil which visually represent the Holy Trinity
Opposite: 1641 does not date the building but is an exercise in numerology

Schloss Hellbrunn, Salzburg

Whatever the weather in Salzburg, go armed with a raincoat or an umbrella when you visit the city's Hellbrunn Gardens. Hellbrunn means clear water, and by name and nature the gardens are a theatrical masterpiece. Completed in 1619, they illustrate the way water framed the evolution of Renaissance design from Humanist to Mannerist, from symmetry to living theatre.

The house and gardens took only fifteen months to create. They were designed by Santino Solari for Markus Sittikus, Count of Hohenems, Archbishop of Salzburg, who had lived and studied Humanism in Italy. He was inspired by the recently rediscovered works of Hero of Alexandria on hydraulics, especially *giochi d'acqua* (water jokes).

Above: The mythical unicorn and an obelisk
Opposite: A shell-encrusted exedra forms the backdrop to the Roman Theatre
Overleaf: Roman wrestlers near the Roman Theatre

Fantasy is played out in the theatres encrusted with shells, stucco, tufa and mirrors in exuberant and humorous Mannerist style. The Neptune Grotto lies beneath the villa, acting as an axis to both garden and emotion. To the north, on one side is a grotto of pleasing frescoes and décor, on the other the Ruined Grotto intended to strike fear into the heart of visitors lest the whole building collapse on them. To the south lies the Grotto of the Songbirds and Mirrors: look outside and be drawn into the garden by the Fountain of Altems. A shell-encrusted exedra (recess) forms the backdrop to the Roman Theatre (*right*), the pool in the foreground leading to the Grotto of Orpheus who

plays his lyre accompanied by water-powered singing birds. In the Roman Theatre there are seats with hidden water jets around a stone banqueting table with a central water channel for cooling wine – something no home should be without!

All the stone for the building was excavated from a quarry on site, its empty crater then fashioned into an amphitheatre with a double archway – the Rock Theatre. How fitting that its opening production on 31 August 1617 was Monteverdi's *Orfeo*, and the first 'open-air' opera north of the Alps. The metal crown on the Crown Grotto lifts up with water pressure, and inside are statues of Apollo flaying Marsyas for having had the temerity to challenge him to a music competition.

Further grottoes have the ubiquitous tableau of Perseus rescuing Andromeda chained to the rock; other more mundane activities include a potter, a miller and a grinder at work. Egyptian history and the River Nile are played out in the Grotto of Cleopatra, sheltered from wild woods by columns with a rising tide of tufa flanked by statuesque fish in niches. The obelisk originated in Egypt and, like the mythical unicorn, was a popular decorative folly in Renaissance gardens.

The words of Dominique Gisberti, court poet to the Prince-Elector Ferdinand Maria of Bavaria, written in 1670, sum up this landscape: 'Hellbrunn is a labyrinth of running water, a playground for water nymphs, a theatre of flowers, a capital of statues, a museum of the Graces.' A playground that will soak you if you don't watch out!

Villa Torrigiani, Camigliano

Olive oil is the symbol of goodness and purity and the Villa Torrigiani, north-east of Lucca, lies in the heart of the land that produces Italy's finest. The villa belonged to the Buonvisi family in the sixteenth century until Nicolao Santini bought it in 1651. Having served as Ambassador for Lucca at the court of Louis XIV in France, returned there looking for an outward expression of his enhanced social standing and wealth. Brimming with fantastic ideas, he set about transforming the Tuscan villa and gardens in the latest French Baroque style which he completed in 1684.

The grand entrance (*opposite*) sets the tone – classical architecture with exuberant ornament. The façade hosts an array of statues in niches right up to the roof pinnacle arranged symmetrically along its balustrades. A majestic avenue of ancient cypresses leads to the high gates which frame the villa. Today the architecture is softened by sweeping lawns, and all that remains of the elaborate Baroque scheme, reputedly designed by Louis XIV's master gardener, André le Nôtre, are the stone-edged basins that would have acted as centrepieces to elaborate geometric *parterres de broderie*. These parterres were laid out to echo the symmetry of the villa façade. To the right of the villa the axis is broken by a circular planted garden which leads to the finest surviving parts – the Garden of Flora and the Fishpond.

Above: A bust in the North Loggia representing one of the Virtues

Opposite: The grand approach

Overleaf: The Garden of Venus

The Garden of Flora is surrounded by high walls and approached by dramatic balustraded double steps punctuated by statuary, from which one descends to a parterre garden defined by clipped box hedging. It recalls the metamorphosis of the green nymph, Chloris, into Flora after the gentle, warm, moist breath of Zephyr had passed over her. The flowerbeds are out-lined with an evergreen framework annually enlivened by the scattering of Botticelli's primavera flowers that herald the flourish and sweet scents of spring. There is a light airy casino in the middle giving fine views over the garden replicated in floral frescoes of roses in urns. Although not introduced until the early nineteenth century, the wisteria provides a flowery canopy. Rather than the ubiquitous lion's mask, an array of crafted spouts decorates the walls from which water pours into a scalloped basin; many are grotesque in appearance and recall those at Bomarzo (pp. 22–7). By comparison the Siren looks very alluring in perpetual song as her double tails entwine her body.

A statue of Flora encircled with wrought-iron masks and flowers watches the seasons from atop the nymphaeum or Grotto of the Winds (the image overleaf of the Garden of Venus is taken from her viewpoint). Statues by the entrance to the grotto

depict the labours of Hercules (p. 44, *below, right*). Stronger winds below are represented by seven statues in seven niches within the cool shade of the nymphaeum; the waterworks created in here were a contemporary wonder. The seven statues of the winds include Aeolus as god of the winds; the chill north wind Boreas who is son of the river god Strymon; Auster for the drying heat of the south, Eurus for the cooling east, and Zephyr, as mentioned above, for the west. The floor is made of black and white pebbles whose swirling pattern is reminiscent of tidal sands. Most unusually there is a statue of Jupiter, thunderbolt to hand, who as god of gods is rarely depicted in gardens. He is flanked by rough-textured, double-tailed tufa sea monsters whose smooth equivalents can be seen at the top of the image of the Fountain of the Organ at the Villa d'Este (p. 33). At his feet a mask that looks like a salivating portrait of his father Saturn is ready to soak you. Beyond the enclosure of Flora's Garden on the other side of the double staircase lies the Fishpond, a mirror of water of the type that inspired rectangular lawns in northern Europe. The flowers in the gardens that surround the Fishpond are in pots around the pool. There are also leafy trees that provide the backdrop to the mythological figures whose statues are placed at intervals on the balustrade and on the pool's edge.

Much of the tree planting throughout the gardens was done in the nineteenth century when most of the geometric formality was removed. The trees provide shade and enclosure, revealing and concealing the garden's boundaries. Throughout the garden *giochi d'acqua* were concealed to surprise passing guests – better to be soaked in warm Italian climes than more northerly ones.

Villa Torrigiani is also known as Villa di Camigliano because camellias were introduced here in the early nineteenth century and are now massed to the left of the villa.

Figures in the Grotto of the Winds
Above, left: Hera
Above, right: Boreas
Below, left: Aeolus
Below, right: Hercules overcomes Hydra, the three-headed monster
Opposite: The interior of the casino delightfully frescoed in tribute to Flora's roses

Herrenhausen, Hanover

The original castle was destroyed in the Second World War but two original pavilions elegantly mark the far corners of the Great Garden at the Herrenhäuser Gärten (Herrenhausen) which, encompassing over 50ha/120 acres, is an exercise in geometric control overlaid with Baroque extravagance. Hanover, historic capital of the Duchy of Hanover, had become the site of the dukes' summer residence in 1665 but it was Sophie, wife of the Elector of Hanover Ernst August and daughter of the exiled Frederick V of the Palatinate, who created the gardens from 1679 onwards.

The Electress Sophie, after despatching her French gardener to Holland for training, transplanted both the reality and the fantasy of her childhood spent in the grand gardens of the Netherlands. Like the great Dutch gardens of Het Loo, Herrenhausen is gardening on the flat and the whole is enclosed by a canal. Extensive avenues of trees line walks the length and breadth of the vast area: in fact, gazing across the axes is an easier option by comparison with the lengthy walks involved in discovering the garden's hidden corners. The *parterres de broderie* – embroidered with branchings and flourishings of clipped box – are coloured brightly by flowers. The Grand Parterre at the centre exudes geometry, order and restraint, with the Bell Fountain, originally furnished with 166 jets, at its core. There are thirty-two elaborate vases and statues of gods, seasons, virtues and continents throughout the garden which, painted bright white, clearly stand out by day or night. The flat topography is more than compensated for by having a fountain that could attain the fantastical height of 35m/115ft in 1721.

The outdoor Hedge Theatre, which was laid out between 1689 and 1692, uses the woods and vistas to provide a dramatic backdrop, a popular Baroque conceit. The stage and approach are lined with extraordinary gilded lead figures posing in dance and dramatic positions. Those en route to the Hedge Theatre and in the wings bring to mind Sally Bowles, *Cabaret* and strains of 'Willkommen, Bienvenue and Welcome'. The originals, of Dutch manufacture, were lined up in 1692 and are undergoing restoration, so bronze copies will continue to act as under-studies until they return to the stage in early 2009. The actual stage is in the shape of a trapezium and the wings are formed from beech hedges. The drama lives on as this is still used for open-air productions.

In 1692 the Electress Sophie acquired land for the New Garden and from 1699 to 1709 it was shaped into long *allées* and *bosquets*, carefully designed to interplay with one another in strictest formality. She died just days before Queen Anne of England so her son became George I and Herrenhausen remained a seventeenth-century timepiece until Georgengarten, a landscaped park on the English model, was created in the nineteenth century. From the Leibniz Temple there are wide views over sweeping lawns and placid lakes framed by carefully arranged copses and specimen trees. In sympathy with their historical surroundings, but not authentic, are the maze and wooden colonnaded temples built to a Dutch design.

Above: One of two matching pavilions

Opposite: The Leibniz Temple in the Georgengarten

Overleaf: Gilded figures line the approach to the Hedge Theatre

Villa Barbarigo Pizzoni Ardemani, Valsanzibio

South-west of Padua at Valsanzibio lies the Villa Barbarigo Pizzoni Ardemani set in a Baroque garden bristling with architectural flights of fantasy and awash with allegorical and moral instruction. It is named after its seventeenth-century creators, Zuane Francesco Barbarigo and his son Antonio, who laid out the gardens from 1669.

Visitors originally arrived by gondola at the Portal of Diana (*overleaf*), an imposing Baroque gateway marking entry into this Edenic fantasy. Diana, calling in her hounds which scale the upper arches, is instantly recognisable by the crescent moon on her head. Leaving the struggles of the world behind, visitors tied their boats to the painted poles and stepped from the vicissitudes of political intrigue in Venice or Padua into the tranquillity of the Garden of Eden.

Described as 'an amphitheatre in the hills', here was a showcase for the creators' collection of antique sculpture which now also shelters over 120 species of trees, most of which were planted in the nineteenth century. The gentler pursuits of botanical and medical research, as well as mechanical and hydraulic innovations, contributed to the garden's pleasures.

In a Baroque interpretation of nature embellished by the hand of man, the gardens are designed along two axes down which water travels, via mirrored fish ponds, cascades and streams, through smooth lawns and between high hedges backed by mature trees. Green, the colour of contemplation, dominates and, as an allegory of the search for self, there is a hedged labyrinth. On the Garena (*left*), an island *conigliera* (rabbit warren), which was restored in the twentieth century by Count Fabio Pizzoni Ardemani, rabbits play a similar role as at Rushton Triangular Lodge (pp. 34–5), but also symbolise divine immanence.

A fountain is dedicated to *fiumi* (streams) and *vento* (wind), but wind in the Aeolian sense, a gentle refreshing breeze. Behind, closest to the woodland, lies Diana's Bath. Emanating from the green shade of Diana's Bath is a path marking the garden's central axis and symbolic core where Pan pipes in the dawn with other gods and nymphs. The small Swan Fountain can be seen in the foreground of the image opposite.

The landscape exudes mystery and obscure mythological references such as in the eight allegorical figures that form a circle around the Fountain of Ecstasy. There are a further sixteen fountains newly restored: the Rainbow Fountain pumps so high that it creates its own rainbow as the sun filters through its mists. On the garden's leafy margins at least seventy statues of mythological characters stand in dappled shade. A climb up the Stairway of Leopards and on to the high ground brings you out at a monument to Time representing the transcendence of human aspiration.

Above: The Garena (Rabbit Island)
Opposite: The symbolic core of the garden, emerging from the green
Overleaf: The Portal of Diana

Palácio da Fronteira, Lisbon

In Benfica, a northern suburb of Lisbon, the Palácio da Fronteira is a folly-filled Portuguese demesne that speaks with an Italian Renaissance accent. Wherever you look the bright *azulejos* or glazed tiles depict classical, satirical and pleasant scenes in their hallmark blue and white. Those in the Battle Room recount the military glories of the palace's founder Dom João de Mascarenhas, 2nd Count of Torre, who was made 1st Marquis of Fronteira in recognition of his valour. His descendants still live here.

If you have ever wondered what constitutes a liberal classical education then follow the *azulejos* along the terrace on the Gallery of the Arts that leads from the palace to the chapel. They depict the seven liberal arts: the primary three, the Trivium, of Rhetorica, Grammatica and Dialectica, and the secondary four, the Quadrivium, of Geometria, Arithmetica, Musica and Astronomia. Musica (*overleaf*) has turned to the fleet-footed Mercury who seems about to leave on a mission. These niches are interspersed with planetary gods such as Diana (Luna), Mars and Apollo (Sol). The crescent moon on Diana represents her planetary status; as goddess of the hunt, she is holding one stag's head in her left hand with another underfoot. The heat of such intellectual activity is lightened by the fantastical scenes on the tiled bench seating – allegories of human conceits portrayed by animals such as monkeys.

Venus, the goddess of all growing things, is well served with shady trees and clipped hedging in the Garden of Venus, and her emergence from the foam celebrated in fountains. Indeed, is it fantastical to ask whether she is associated with the man in diving spectacles in one of the *azulejos*? Like the Salle de Fraîcheur at the Château d'Urfé (pp. 18–21), the Casa de Fresco at Fronteira provides respite from the summer's heat with its shell- and china-lined grotto interior, but with Venus presiding its message here is purely sensual.

Above: Diana as planetary goddess Luna
Opposite: The Gallery of the Kings

As its name implies the Jardim Grande is a magnificent geometric parterre of box (*Buxus* spp.) clipped into interlocking squares, diamonds, stars and wedges, with roses providing scent and symbolism. Athletic, graceful statues rise above the patterned hedging, beyond which lies the Galeria dos Reis (Gallery of the Kings), mirrored in the waters of the tank. There are also twelve knights forever prancing depicted in *azulejos* (*opposite*) – according to legend they went to England to joust for twelve English maidens. In the courtly manner of the garden, the fifteen Portuguese kings are framed in exquisite *azulejos* of pineapples in blue and lustred bronze. And so you ascend and descend elegantly via a balustraded staircase.

Gallery of the Arts

Bramham Park, Wetherby

In 1697 Robert Benson returned from a Grand Tour of Europe with a grand plan for his estate near Wetherby in Yorkshire. His study of Italian architecture and French gardens inspired the creation over the next thirteen years of one of the last great geometric gardens in England. Of all the folly landscapes in this book, Bramham must rank as the gentlest tickle of intellectual and visual fancy.

Straight canals and avenues radiated across the landscape in a pattern known as *pattes d'oie* or goosefoot – a splendidly descriptive term. The powerful use of avenues and water to draw in the countryside whilst at the same time stretching out to exert the influence of the mansion on its surroundings was perfected by the supremo of Baroque French garden design, Le Nôtre.

There appears to be a Benson family network: the probably related William Benson also came from Yorkshire and his sister married Henry Hoare at Stourhead (pp. 90–5). He was skilled in engineering and became Surveyor General (replacing Christopher Wren) and designed the fountains at Herrenhausen (pp. 46–9). His literary connections also bridged the Baroque and 'landscape style' philosophy; he championed John James's translation of A.J. Dézalliers d'Argenville's dramatically formal and geometric *La Théorie et pratique du jardinage* whose designs for woodland are echoed at Bramham, and translated Virgil's *Georgics* which inspirationally

Above: The octagonal Gothic Temple
Opposite: The Rotunda with the Obelisk dedicated to Robert Lane-Fox

celebrated the myth and politics of agriculture. Finally his Wiltshire domain at Wilbury shares many design characteristics with Bramham, such as an avenue of beech trees lining the path to an octagonal temple.

In the hilly wooded 365ha/900 acre terrain of Bramham Park, Robert Benson achieved a setting that appreciated the Baroque and anticipated the so-called landscape style. Although there was a formal parterre near the house, he did not raze the ground to billiard-table flatness but adapted the formality of the inner 28ha/70 acres to natural contours, bounded by a ha-ha which provided both a fashionable bastion against animals and fine prospects. So the avenues strike out asymmetrically from a wood around the house into two large woods across the park while providing long straight vistas from it; by contrast within the woodland areas he created sinuous paths. The *allées* of beech trees lead into *salles de verdure* ('green rooms') that act as intersections and settings for statues, and were the result of collaboration between Benson and John Wood the Elder of Bath. Wood arrived in the early 1720s and in 1728 drew up a detailed survey of the (almost unchanged) layout.

One of the sources in the far south-west that fed the ingenious system of pipes for the water features was marked by a rustic grotto. A boat trip up the T-shaped canal offered incidental fishing and panoramic views from the bastion at the far end. This canal acted as a *miroir d'eau* and supplied water to the Cascades, Queen's Hollow and the semi-circular *bassin* in the parterre.

Benson was MP for York, Chancellor of the

Exchequer, British Ambassador to Spain and in recognition was made Lord Bingley. The avenues planted by him through the Yorkshire woods lasted until devastating storms in 1962. He created a setting for his daughter Harriet and her husband George Lane-Fox, later 2nd Lord Bingley, to raise a proliferation of temples that would elegantly terminate the vistas. Near the house Harriet commissioned a temple by James Paine that was first used as an orangery and then as a garden house; between 1906 and 1914, when the architect Detmar Blow directed extensive renovations, it was consecrated and is now known as The Chapel. Paine also designed the Tuscan or Open Temple at the westernmost point of the original gardens, which was constructed to shelter foolish walkers caught in the rain.

The Gothic Temple, also attributed to him, is a carbon copy of plate 57 in Batty Langley's 1747 *Gothic Architecture Improved* that duplicated James Gibbs's 1729 *A Book of Architecture*. The water that gushes from the mouths of dragons in the five pools in the Obelisk Pond and Cascades series is lined up across the Broad Walk to Black Fen and Paine's Ionic Round Temple, probably inspired by the Temple of Ancient Virtues at Stowe (pp. 64–9). Beyond this towers the 30m/100ft Obelisk at the core of ten rides which was erected in memory of Harriet and George Lane-Fox's son, Robert.

There is nothing discreet about the ha-ha – it is a massive terrace walk that offers the spectacle of the wider park and its classical architectural follies. Five high beech avenues lead to the Four Faces Urn that stands some 6m/20ft high and depicts the four seasons. It may be folly but family tradition advises walking three times around the urn one way, and three the other, stopping and making a wish.

CLASSICISM & GRANDEUR

In Europe the eighteenth century dawned in thrall to the splendour of Baroque architecture and its controlled perfection of nature. Baroque became a symbol of absolute monarchy and Catholicism: it emanated from the Sun King, Louis XIV, by way of his landscape designer, André Le Nôtre, and with Versailles as exemplar.

In Anglican England tastes were changing: nature shaped the landscape, implying the naturalness of the country's political institutions. The vogue for neoclassicism signalled an adoption of Palladian architecture as the new English vernacular; however, ruins were more interesting because they evoked the grandeur of the past.

Later, Lancelot 'Capability' Brown simplified and codified English landscaping, and we can see this translated into the countless *jardins anglais* that litter Europe and beyond.

Stowe, Buckingham

Stowe near Buckingham provides classic evidence of how the Baroque parterres of England were swept first

into intellectual theatre by William Kent and then into the beautiful formulaic intelligence of Lancelot 'Capability' Brown. The motto of the patron, Sir Richard Temple, Whig grandee and general, *Templa quam dilecta*, should be on your lips as you enter. How beautiful are thy temples? This is beauty in the sense of delight and generator of pleasure not just a pun on the family name. The temple exemplar is furthered in over thirty architectural extravagances including bridges, castle, grottoes, monuments, alcoves, ruins, baths and arches.

Above: Grenville's rostral column
Opposite: The Oxford Bridge
Overleaf: The Temple of British Worthies

When Sir Richard was elevated to Viscount Cobham in 1718 Stowe was laid out in Baroque splendour, including the Temple of Venus, an expression of erotic love, designed by John Vanbrugh. However, fifteen years later Cobham was outraged by the 1733 Excise Bill of the upstart Prime Minister Sir Robert Walpole, and later commemorated him as a headless statue in the now lost Temple of Modern Virtue. Kent, theatre designer and painter, was commissioned to dramatically landscape Old Whig political values into architectural manifestations, with

the park as stage and the temples and monuments as players accompanied by choral refrains to medieval and Saxon virtues, friendship, valour and independence. The approach over the rustic Oxford Bridge (*opposite*) was probably inspired by the Roman bridge over the River Bacchiglione in Vicenza.

Through a Doric arch the visitor glimpses Kent's masterpiece of allusion – a look-alike Temple of Vesta, actually the Temple of Ancient Virtue, above Elysian Fields crossed by a limpid stream, with a distant Palladian Bridge. The water acts as mirror to the Temple of British Worthies with a niche in the centre for Mercury who guides souls through the Elysian Fields and an inscription to a faithful friend on the back. To the right are eight representatives of traditional Whig ideals of political and military action including King Alfred, Queen Elizabeth I and King William III; to the left, eight men of letters, thought and architecture such as Alexander Pope, Inigo Jones who first introduced Palladian designs into England, John Milton and William Shakespeare. The faithful friend Signor Fido on the back was Cobham's dog.

Across the water the sixteen worthies (*overleaf*) look up to the sixteen columns of the Temple of Ancient Virtue – pillars of society? They are Roman in design but contain four Greek heroic statues: the poet, Homer, the philosopher, Socrates, the law-giver, Lycurgus, and the soldier, Epaminondas. Temple prized England's political liberty and looked to Greece as the home of democracy and liberty, whereas Rome had been

Above: The Chinese House

Opposite, top: The Palladian Bridge

Opposite, below: James Gibbs's Gothic Temple

victorious at the expense of freedom. The original statues were sold in 1921 and are now at Cottesbrooke Hall in Northamptonshire. Across the landscape, the Palladian Bridge (*opposite, above*) exudes classic elegance as it spans the sinuous lake whose reflections sparkle on the mansion's decorative ceilings. Nearby the Chinese House (*above*), with recumbent Chinese lady, is reputedly the earliest in England (noted in 1738). It used to be by an old pond complete with 'Figures of two Chinese Birds about the Size of a Duck, which move with the Wind as if alive'.

Alfred, the Saxons and the Gothic style represent the roots of English liberty, loudly proclaimed in perhaps Stowe's greatest folly, James Gibbs's Gothic Temple (*opposite, below*), which is dedicated to the 'Liberty of Our Ancestors' and inscribed with 'Thank God I am not a Roman'. In a delectable paradox Gibbs, a Scots Roman Catholic and Tory who had perfected the Baroque style, designed it using a triangular plan in defiance of the classical square and circle. Robustly built in Northamptonshire ironstone with a distant echo of Rushton Triangular Lodge (pp. 34–5) and inspiration for Wörlitz, near Dessau, the ground plan and the group of three windows allude to the Whig ideals of Liberty, Enlightenment and the Constitution:

a clear statement of Protestant (think Elizabeth I and William III) individuality against Roman Catholic (Jacobite) conformity, and constitutional monarchy against absolutism and divine right. Gibbs also designed the Boycott Pavilions, one of which housed the gardener Woodward for much of the eighteenth century.

By 1741, when Kent employed the young Lancelot Brown, the landscape at Stowe was positively littered with temples and dramatic follies that invited intellectual gymnastics. In 1747 Cobham's nephew, Captain Thomas Grenville, died. A rostral column (p. 64) was erected with a Muse on the top holding a scroll from which she can only read of heroic deeds, that is, the death of Captain Grenville. It has the inscription 'The Muse forbids Heroic Worth to die'. Brown's own developing style is serenely displayed in the Grecian Valley and Temple of Concord and Victory. After ten years 'Capability' Brown left to stamp his hallmark formulaic intelligence across England, a formula emulated as the *jardin anglais* across Europe and into Russia.

In 1921 Stowe was sold to become a school and the Grand Avenue was divided into building plots. Clough Williams-Ellis (*see* Portmeirion, pp. 188–93) was appointed architect and in a grand personal gesture he bought and saved the Grand Avenue.

Villa Palagonia, Bagheria

When Goethe visited Villa Palagonia during his Italian travels in 1787, he wrote that this 'Villa of Monsters' was in 'bad taste and [the] folly of an eccentric mind'. The chairs' seats sloped forward and the velvet cushioned backs were studded with spikes to deter people from lolling. A dreamless sleep was unlikely in the company of the menagerie of huge snakes, lizards, spiders and scorpions sculpted in coloured marble that decorated the bedroom. Finally, lost for words to describe the array of eccentricities, he coined the word 'palagonian', which came to be used to define the Sicilian love of the fantastic.

Villa Palagonia is the most remarkable of the Baroque country villas that litter this rugged Tyrrhenian Coast. The great and the good of eighteenth-century Palermo loved to be beside the seaside and nearby Bagheria fulfilled their desire. Here Prince Francesco Ferdinando Palagonia Gravina started building his villa in 1715 and in 1749 his hunchbacked grandson, also Francesco, 7th Prince of Palagonia, took on the mantle of eccentricity, adding the decorative follies that punctuate the encircling walls and gates (*overleaf*).

The grounds surrounding the villa are long gone but the building remains, its concave façade exuding a gracious Baroque grandeur with a double balustraded staircase (*right*) leading up to the *piano nobile* or first floor. Designed on a central axis that runs from outer wall to outer wall, the villa's fanned ground plan, aligned with the avenue, looks like a deck of cards and is enclosed by double walls which almost form a quatrefoil around it. The plans were drawn up by Tommaso Maria Napoli who was both a Dominican monk and military engineer attached to the Senate of Palermo as an assistant architect.

The villa's elliptical entrance hall that celebrates the Labours of Hercules in lively frescoes leads to the vast ballroom or Hall of Mirrors, which fulfils any dream (or nightmare) of marbled halls, the walls lined with fine marble, crystal, coloured glass and polychrome marble busts of the Palagonia family (p. 75). The busts were dressed as though alive and their arms stretched out into the room – catching your attention in every sense. Forty obelisks and columns have thrown off their classical constructional shackles by being cemented towers of teapots, cups, saucers and chandeliers, one column rising majestically from a chamber pot. With your feet firmly planted on the geometric patterned three-dimensional marble floor, start to circle and engage in the folly of looking up at the angled mirrors. Savour the visual horrors into which you are distorted.

A rectangular chapel with a small campanile is built into the walls, inside which a kneeling man is suspended on a chain that has been screwed into the centre of a

Above: The main staircase

Opposite: A palagonian figure

Overleaf: A monstrous regiment caps the walls and the entrance gates

painting of Christ. Was this man Francis of Assisi or, as Goethe wrote, simply the 'symbol of the relentless piety of the Prince'? The prince belonged to the Order of the Fathers of Mercy and raised funds, sometimes by begging, to release ransomed prisoners. A bust shows the face and breasts of a beautifully dressed woman being eaten away by scorpions, centipedes, earthworms and moths – curiously predating the ants in Salvador Dalí's film *Un chien andalou* and so many of his paintings.

The medley of six hundred assorted statues on the encircling walls and gates of Villa Palagonia were sculpted out of the local Aspra tufa. Among them are five- and six-headed monsters, Punchinellos surrounded by serpents, donkeys standing up on their hind legs and wearing ties, neatly bibbed lions consuming oysters, ostriches in hooped skirts, warriors, musicians, lords and ladies, hunchbacks, dragons and other sundry mythological beasts. These grotesques bear a marked resemblance to the tribal or totem signs used by the original inhabitants of Sicily which survived as tokens of good luck and as protectors from the evil eye. These actually fairly benign-looking monsters jostle for your attention in groups around the walls and over the two entrance gates. Rather than carrying the weight of the heavens on his shoulders, Atlas is carrying a barrel. Goethe reported that the gates had a statue of a dwarf with the head of a laurel-garlanded Roman emperor riding on a dolphin and a thorn-garlanded emperor with two noses.

However, the monsters were expensive and the prince's family and heirs tried to restrain him and eventually the king was required to intervene.

In 1885 the Castronovo family acquired the villa and it is still owned by their descendants. Villa Palagonia is exceptional in that it is open to the public, unlike the other privately owned Baroque country villas that litter Bagheria.

Above, left: A gargoyle water spout
Above, right: Detail of a mythological fresco
Below, left: A polychrome marble bust of one of the Palagonia family
Below, right: A grotesque providing protection from the evil eye
Opposite: The ballroom

La Granja de San Ildefonso, Segovia

Nestling in the foothills of the Sierra Guadarrama near Segovia, this is no poor man's Versailles: the palace may be smaller but the gardens that move between Baroque and Rococo are rich in sculptures and fantastic fountains, in a setting of geometric precision. As a grandson of Louis XIV, Philip V, King of Spain and the Indies, had spent his childhood and youth in the Baroque splendour of the French court until he ascended the Spanish throne aged seventeen in 1700. He carried French ideas and artists to Spain – visions of Versailles, Marly and the network of 'crown jewels' that surrounded Paris, brought to their zenith by the landscaping vision of André le Nôtre and the flamboyant interior and sculptural designs of Charles le Brun.

La Granja's landscape design was by René Carlier and the sculptures by René Frémin, a student of François Girardon, whose sculptures had adorned Versailles and Marly, and also Jean Thierry, one of his associates. Unlike Versailles, water and water power were not a problem, so the grandeur of the fountains, whether in action or at rest, matches anything in Europe. The dramatic mountains that terminate the vista from the gardens also provided the crystal streams gushing with cut-glass quality. Carlier tamed the streams into the Ria in a series of cascades and stepped waterfalls whose progress can be viewed from a raised terrace. The marble steps of the Monumental Cascade topped by the Pavilion (p. 79, *below*) have strong echoes of Marly.

Behind the palace a central *parterre de broderie* provides an intricate green earthy frame to the cascade and Fountain of Amphitrite, goddess of the sea, who was the daughter of Nereus and Doris and consort of Poseidon. The scheme culminates in the Fountain of the Three Graces. To one side, the Grove of the Winds is aesthetically controlled by the presence of the Aeolus Fountain, Aeolus being the god of the wind (*see* Villa Torrigiani, pp. 40–5). To the other side is a living ode to water, known as the Horse Race, in which, looking from the palace, you see the delicate Fountains of the Shells and the Fan, composed of a water nymph holding a fish from whose mouth water issues in a fan shape. She is accompanied by zephyrs, those moist gods of the west wind that help the garden flower.

Above: The Fall of Moorish Soldiers from the Fountain of Fame

Opposite: The Latona Basin

In the Neptune Fountain (p. 79, *above*) the sea god rises from the waters on a shell-encrusted carriage, pulled at high speed by hippocamps (horses with shells for hooves) and accompanied by all manner of jetting tritons, cupids and fishes. A large mask spouts water, representing two of Spain's key rivers, in the Pond of the Ebro and Segre. Then the Apollo Fountain rises grandly, demonstrating his power over the serpent Python whilst the amorino of art offers him a laurel wreath and the amorino of war an arrow. Minerva holds out an olive branch to Apollo in recognition of the peace he has won by vanquishing Envy and Discord.

Above, left: The Fountain of Fame
sounding her watery trumpet
Above, right: The Baths of Diana
Below, left: The Pavilion
Below, right: Nymphs in the
Baths of Diana
Opposite, top: The Neptune
Fountain and Cascade
Opposite, below: The marble steps
of the Monumental Cascade

So on to further virtuous heights, beyond the Half Moon pool, to the crescendo of Andromeda's Fountain. There is the hapless Andromeda, chained to a rock by her father, about to be devoured by a sea dragon when her saviour, Perseus, risks all to kill the dragon and release her. The Fountain of Fame (p. 77) mounted on Pegasus triumphantly sounds her watery trumpet as the slain fall into the four main rivers of Spain. The sculptural detail on the fountains, such as the fall of the Moorish soldiers beaten by Fame, is as glorious without water as it is with it.

The domination of water at La Granja is calmed by the symmetry of the Andromeda parterres – an iconographic journey that heralds Philip's own operatic role as saviour of the monarchy, vanquisher of the enemies in the War of the Spanish Succession, dispeller of Envy and Discord and patron of the arts. In this setting modesty would be a fatal folly.

The Latona Basin (p. 76) recalls Versailles and the protection afforded to Louis XIV during his childhood by his mother, paralleled in the classical world by Latona, mother of Apollo and Diana, who fended off jeering Lycian peasants so as to give her children water. Jupiter punished the Lycian peasants for their cruelty by turning them into frogs, delightfully portrayed here in various stages of metamorphosis – a narrative font of noble Latona, screaming peasants, their transitional stages and finally spitting frogs.

The Baths of Diana (*above, right*) terminate one lateral vista and appropriately back on to the woods beyond, but this is very far from a sylvan scene. It is a hydraulic wonder, not completed until 1745 some forty-five years after Philip's arrival. Diana rests from hunting in her Baroque-meets-Rococo shell-incrusted niche, with five nymphs to wash her, dry her and brush her hair. The other nymphs frolic with dogs and dolphins that spray fine jets into the air. Actaeon watches whilst playing the flute, captured for ever in innocent safety.

Wentworth Woodhouse, Rotherham

The traffic that thunders along the M1 past Rotherham in Yorkshire is within a few miles of an idyllic landscape scattered with follies, and the longest country house façade in England. The follies are an overt expression of familial rivalry and True Whig aggrandisement that parallel respectively the sentiments of the Jealous Wall at Belvedere House (pp. 116-17) and the Old Whig outpourings at Stowe (pp. 64-9). This estate was the rightful inheritance of Thomas Wentworth but to his disgust it was willed to his cousin Thomas Watson-Wentworth. The deadly sin of envy engendered a bitter rivalry in Wentworth who vented his spleen by purchasing the nearby Stainsborough estate, building prodigiously and renaming it Wentworth Castle. Watson-Wentworth, later 1st Marquess of Rockingham, took up the challenge with gusto, as did his son Charles. Thus the extensive and profitable estate of Wentworth Woodhouse was dotted by architectural exclamation marks. Rival cultural display was as dominant inside as out: when four marble copies of famous statues were displayed at Wentworth Castle, eight were commissioned from Massimiliano Soldani Benzi for Wentworth Woodhouse.

How should an enlightened Whig's landscape look? A cultural display of classical grandeur fuelled by commercial profit – folly juxtaposed with practical enlightenment. This was successfully achieved through investment in agriculture and coalmining, an infrastructure of canals, and farms and housing for estate workers. West meets east at the Wentworth Woodhouse mansion whose Baroque façade was started by Watson-Wentworth in 1724. Work began on the west and continued until 1749 when the Palladian east front was completed, thus creating a prodigious building 185m/606ft long which covered some 1.2ha/3 acres. In 1768 James Carr, the York architect who designed Harewood House, was called in to design Palladian stables to the north of the house around a magnificent central fountain with a riding school and housing for estate workers. So west, east, north, this extravagant bastion of grandeur was completed by the great south terrace wall curving around the base of an Ionic temple.

Directly north of the house stands the pyramidal Needle's Eye (p. 82, *above*, *right*), topping 14.5m/48ft with a flamboyant urn, its base arched into an elegant ogee. According to legend its name is derived from a bet that the 2nd Marquess of Rockingham could drive a coach and galloping horses through the eye of a needle. He was a noted gambler, having wagered £500 on a Norwich to London race between five turkeys and five geese. The folly of his words took the form of a folly that would leave him undefeated but presumably out of pocket. (Incidentally, camels can pass through the eye of the needle as the original

Above: One of the lodges to the park, the Ionic Temple and the south terraced wall

Opposite: The Rockingham Monument

Above, left: The Needle's Eye

Above, right: The Saxon Tower, a former windmill

Below, left: The Doric Temple

Below, right: The Hoober Stand

Opposite: Nollekens's life-size statue of Charles, 2nd Marquess of Rockingham

'camel' is a type of rope.) What is certain is that it provided a carriageway between Wentworth and the North Lodge near Brampton, and an elegant adjunct to the park landscape that extended to 600ha/1,500 acres.

Further east is the first of three English triangular prospect towers designed by Henry Flitcroft for Whig patrons. The Hoober Stand (*below, right*) is a pyramidal folly celebrating the defeat of 'a most Unnatural Rebellion' at Culloden in 1746 (the battle marked the end of a sixty year civil war for succession after which 'Bonnie' Prince Charlie escaped and went into exile in France) and Watson-Wentworth being elevated to 1st Marquis of Rockingham by George II. The three sides have rounded corners, and it soars to over 30m/100ft in smoke-blackened yellow-stone, offering a vista over the fruits of peace after a just war – an arcadia of rural sport and productivity. In 1765 Flitcroft designed Alfred's Tower at Stourhead (*see* pp. 90–5) to commemorate the victorious conclusion of the Seven Years' War.

Towering 4.5m/15ft higher than the Hoober Stand, the Tuscan order Keppel's Column celebrates Admiral Augustus Keppel, a hero of the Seven Years' War, who then opposed war in the American colonies and fought to defend against invasion by the French. Enemies closer to home tried to dishonour him but he was exonerated after a lengthy court martial; in celebration Wentworth Woodhouse was illuminated, guns were fired, a hogshead of ale donated and a party held for 10,000 people.

Carr was retained as architectural consultant for almost fifty years, his climactic eye-catcher and last edifice being the elegant three-storeyed neoclassical Rockingham Monument erected in 1788 (p. 81). It was designed as a mausoleum 'not to entertain the eye, but to instruct the mind'. In good folly fashion its sole purpose has been to entertain the eye as Rockingham was buried in York Minster.

CHARLES WATSON WENTWORTH,
MARQUISS OF ROCKINGHAM, EARL OF MALTON,
VISCOUNT HIGHAM OF HIGHAM FERRERS,
BARON OF ROCKINGHAM, MALTON, WATH, AND
HARROWDEN AND BARONET, IN GREAT BRITAIN,
EARL AND BARON OF MALTON IN THE
KINGDOM OF IRELAND, LORD LIEUTENANT AND

Jardines de Aranjuez, Madrid

There is an old steam train that runs from Madrid south to the Palace of Aranjuez, taking its passengers from the pent-up city to a man-made paradise. Again and again it is referred to as the Spanish royal family's exclusive Garden of Eden where they would spend every spring – annually refreshed by nature's reawakening. Water is the font of life and its plentiful presence is thanks to the grandly meandering River Tagus, the source of visual and aural effects around the palace which dates back to 1387. To devise an itinerary around Eden would seem akin to folly – the extensive gardens here branched out and blossomed anew over the centuries, offering settings for elaborate architectural extravagances. However, east of this Eden lie landscaped gardens divided from the west by a loop in the meandering river which provides the palace's northerly outlook and offers a gentle means of travel to both. The functional buildings and business of reality lie to the south.

There was once a series of secret enclosed gardens close to the palace designed for royal privacy, one of which survives as a decorative parterre, appropriately known as the King's Garden (1582). Here, aligned with the palace are three fountains, the first dedicated to the Nereids and the next to Ceres, and finally the dominant Fountain of Hercules and Antaeus (*overleaf*) on top of which the hero is portrayed in a death struggle with the African (Libyan) giant Antaeus, son of Gaia (Terra) and Poseidon (Neptune). Water jets from the mouth of Antaeus whilst scenes of Hercules' earlier successes are portrayed around the plinth. The embroidered parterre

design is French-inspired, in keeping with the influence of Philip V (*see* La Granja, pp. 76–9), and was first planted for his visit to Aranjuez in 1737. The Baroque parterres were reinterpreted in the nineteenth century but the flowery, ordered sense remains.

The western loop in the great River Tagus and the smaller Picotajo forms the grand and extensive Island Garden (built by Philip II in 1561). In high formal style, it was conceived on a strong central axis from which a series of Renaissance-inspired compartments, each containing parterres, was created. The build-up of sediment from the Tagus was so great that, by 1729, Philip V was able to create a further parterre on the long peninsula named Isleta. In the eighteenth century the axis was lined with trees and much of the planting lost, but most of the fountains survived. Two of the bridges and gateways created for the exclusive use of the monarchs still exist, the latter consisting of four Ionic pillars on a plinth surmounted by putti tending flower urns – 'Jardin del' appears on the cornice of one and 'Principe' on the other (p. 88, *above*, *right*).

East of the palace is the contrasting and extensive Prince's Garden, a *jardin anglais*, which retained the Spring Orchard, its northerly margins bounded by the river. There are elaborate landing stages on the upper bend of the river, decorated with picturesque pavilions (*opposite*), plus a further recreational pavilion on the far side of the river. Architectural interest was generated

Above: The Bacchus Fountain

Opposite: The Chinese Pavilion

Overleaf: The Hercules and Antaeus Fountain

Above, left: The Ionic Temple
Above, right: A pillar for the
royal gateway
Below, left: Figures supporting
the Fountain of Narcissus in
the Prince's Garden
Below, right: Hercules stays
the Hydra
Opposite: The Casa del Laborador

by the Fortìn or Little Fort which held a battery of small cannons that fired salutes as the royal barges passed along the Tagus. A 'Castle' was built to provide a belvedere or 'mirador' from which to enjoy views over the landscape further upstream. The gardener Paul Boutelou extended the easterly reaches by designing a series of landscape gardens that flow sinuously between the established features. Halfway down is the only architectural fountain: a beautiful Apollo with consummately sculpted drapery which is framed in a columned exedra topped by peacocks. It was part of Queen Christina of Sweden's collection in Rome that was acquired by Philip V in 1724 and originally intended for La Granja (pp. 76–9). Carlos IV decided to display it here at Aranjuez, although what we see today is a copy. Nearby, the Chinese Garden is an *anglo-chinois* interpretation of the classic lake and island pattern and the banks of the lake are an exercise in irregularity – a mass of tiny inlets and projections. The Ionic Temple (*above, left*) contrasts with the elaborate Chinese Pavilion (p. 84), both seemingly on floating platforms, a Chinese stone boat or gondola 'moored' on the water and an obelisk made out of oriental hazelnut granite raised on rocks. The classical temple's ten green columns had been brought from La Granja so that the architect Juan de Villanueva could incorporate them in his design; it originally sheltered a collection of Egyptian idols, also from Queen Christina's collection – a splendid mixed metaphor.

At the furthest end of the landscape is the Casa del Laborador (Worker's Cottage) (*opposite*), a mini-palace lined with Roman-style busts. It was finished in 1803, and expressed an echo of Versailles in fulfilling Carlos IV's notion of a *petit trianon* where he could entertain on a modest scale; rather than set near a contrived rivulet, it was originally virtually moated by the river. Beyond it lies the Miraflores Park where nature has regained a less than Edenic control.

Stourhead, Stourton

Lying in the rolling hills of Wiltshire, within striking distance of the classical elegance of Bath, the sublime landscape at Stourhead echoes Aeneas's journey to found Rome. Its creator, banker Henry Hoare II, had a grand plan: the architecture of Andrea Palladio would provide the model for the buildings, while inspiration for the mythic landscapes would come from paintings he had seen on his three-year Grand Tour, most of it spent in Italy. His dream was to create a series of living tableaux like those by Nicolas Poussin, Claude Lorrain and Gaspard Dughuet as well as conjuring up the stormy scenes painted by Salvator Rosa: all inspirational in imposing the Roman Campagna on to English estates. Full of nuances and symbolism, Hoare's landscaping journey would be understood and appreciated by those who had had the benefit of a classical education.

Stourhead Hall was designed in neoclassical Palladian style by Colen Campbell, porticoed and built of carefully masoned stone, but the entrance to the grounds by contrast is through the original rough-hewn Gothic gatehouse. In eighteenth-century landscape style, grass grows right up to the door so that the hall grazes in its beautiful surroundings. The grounds fall away offering a grand tour of revealed and concealed classical follies around the margins of a naturalistic man-made lake with gently wind-pleated waters. St Peter's Pump was erected over the first springs of the Stour in Six Wells Bottom.

It was only after reading Voltaire that Hoare discovered his admiration for Alfred the Great, the

English king who had orchestrated the triumph of native culture and freedom over foreign invaders. Still visible to the north-west, although some 3km/2 miles away, is the triangular 'Alfred's Tower' on Kingsettle Hill built to outdo his friend Charles Hamilton's at Painshill. At 50m/160ft high, it is a massively solid tribute to Alfred the Great designed by Henry Flitcroft who had already worked to such heights at Wentworth Woodhouse (pp. 80–3). On this spot in 879 AD King Alfred emerged from hiding to raise his standard and to drive back and defeat the Danes. One other massive landmark, before embarking in the footsteps of Virgil's Aeneas, is the long avenue which frames the sun-topped Obelisk (not the original) (*right*), representative of the sun and all its powers.

In England 'classical' equated to Virgil, whose love of nature and craftsmanship had inspired John Milton's *Paradise Lost*, which in turn prefigures eighteenth-century Edenic landscape ideals. A natural spring provided the site for the first garden building, the Temple of Flora (*opposite*), swathed in evergreens and inscribed with words from Virgil's *Aeneid*: 'Procul, O procul este, profani' – Keep away, anyone profane, keep away – spoken by the Cumaean Sybil to Aeneas as he entered the Underworld. The classically inspired

Above: The sun-topped Obelisk
Opposite: The Temple of Flora
Overleaf: The Pantheon and Turf Bridge

Above: Alfred's Tower

Opposite: The Nymph
of the Grotto

temple was designed by Henry Flitcroft, and provides a flowery view across to the Pantheon (*previous page*) inspired by Claude Lorrain's *Landscape with Aeneas at Delos*. The route follows the margins of the sinuous lake, the journey punctuated with ever-changing classical vistas; the highest point crowned by the Temple of Apollo offers a goal to aspire to. The voyage in and out of light, deep and dappled shade is thanks to later tree planting, especially by Hoare's grandson Richard Colt Hoare. Today's backdrop of colour provides a further painterly magic that would have delighted Poussin.

In *The Aeneid* Virgil described how Aeneas and his men take refuge in a sea cave near Carthage. At Stourhead the earth suddenly opens up to offer an easy descent into the grotto or *Nympharum domus*, an inscribed quotation from Virgil acting as a gentle reminder: 'Easy the descent to hell but to find your way back up to the air, that is the hardest task.' Help is at hand in this dark underworld of rough-hewn stone — light filters in through a rocky aperture to illuminate the recumbent body of a nymph (*opposite*) whilst

offering stunning glimpses out across the lake. This sleeping nymph was based on a statue of Ariadne in the Vatican: the words cut in the marble below her are Alexander Pope's translation of a pseudo-classical fifteenth-century poem much used in Italian Renaissance fountains:

> *Nymph of the grot these sacred springs I keep*
> *And to the murmur of these waters sleep;*
> *Ah spare my slumbers gently tread the cave,*
> *And drink in silence or in silence lave.*

Glimmering at the end of the grotto chambers, stepping from the cooling waters, the river god Tiber raises his hand in greeting and ushers you back up the steep steps to the virtuous light. The forefinger of his raised hand points in the direction of the Pantheon. Tiber is a stunningly powerful figure that bears an extraordinary resemblance to the figure of Tiber in Salvator Rosa's engraving *The Dream of Aeneas*. You emerge into the realms of light and continue the journey of enlightenment. The Gothic Cottage serves as a 'native English' reminder before the classical Pantheon explodes into view. The Pantheon in name and in appearance is directly inspired by the original built for the Emperor Hadrian in Rome, and it provides a magnificent setting from which to look out at and admire this grand classical landscape. Hercules dominates the interior, resting in Farnese style after his labours but with the English inspiration of the bulging biceps of a contemporary prize-fighter, Jack Broughton. Apart from Hercules, this Pantheon includes many Roman gods and Christian figures representing virtue, fertility, passion and hunting, emotions that beat in the breast of the widower Hoare. There is the god of wine, Bacchus, who also rescued Ariadne, and through wine's good offices civilised discussion; the Callipygian Venus who rejoices in the alternative name of the 'Venus of the beautiful buttocks'; and then there are Diana, Flora, Meleager, Isis, St Susanna and Livia Augusta, who evoke hunting, flowers and feminine virtue.

Across the water beyond the turfed Palladian Bridge is the Bristol High Cross which was bought in 1764, after it had been declared 'a ruinous and superstitious Relick, which is at present a public nuisance', and rebuilt to form a pleasing Gothic architectural accent. Framed with the parish church, it also draws the mind away from pagan to Christian associations.

Departure from the Pantheon means that, like Hercules, we have to make the classic choice between the stony, uphill path of virtue (to the Temple of Apollo) or the easier 'primrose' path of pleasure (staying alongside the lake). Virtue has its rewards: they are here at the Temple of Apollo and its exquisite Corinthian columns which shelter a large cast of the Belvedere Apollo. The sun god is illuminated by gilded and real solar rays from the dome. Inspired by a circular temple at Baalbec, it provides stunning views to the mortal world below.

Schloss Schwetzingen, Schwetzingen

The extensive grounds of Schloss Schwetzingen exercise the mind and body in a challenging programme of follies bristling with overt and cryptic symbolism. With powerful Masonic associations, interpretation is on many levels – classical mythological, Christian mystical, scientific and aristocratic.

Above: The Stag Fountain
Opposite: The Temple of Apollo

The aristocrat behind these grand schemes was the Elector Carl Theodor, who succeeded to the Palatinate throne in 1743. A classical seal of approval is carefully sited in the gardens in the Temple of Minerva, originally with work by the artist Gabriel de Grupello. There are two rows of eight columns through which you enter the temple interior to pay homage to Minerva, the ancient Roman goddess of wisdom, technical skill and invention. She is depicted on the temple frieze leaning on a shield complete with a Gorgon's head and the plan of the park laid out in front of her. Carl Theodor had engaged the architect Nicolas de Pigage whose first project was to extend the summer palace by adding two long, curving wings. This semicircle is mirrored by a grand circular parterre enclosed by trellised walks, with vast avenues radiating from the centre that lead to a host of marvels, not least an architectural representation in four stages of the cycle of day and night – birth, death and rebirth. Dawn is represented by the Bathhouse that leads to the new day of the Temple of Apollo which sets into the dusk of the Temple of Mercury and enters night in the Mosque.

Iconographically, the Bathhouse (dawn) is the most intriguing. Its ground plan closely replicates the female reproductive organs. This association is emphasised by three symbols of female sexuality: *Muschel* or shells (*Muschi* is a German slang term for female genitalia); amethysts the colour of sexually excited genitalia; and the aviaries of birds because *Vögel* sounds like *vögeln*, the German for sexual intercourse. We have to make the journey from the birth canal into the world for the dawn of our existence and the painting on the Bathhouse ceiling is 'Aurora dislodges the night'.

Day is the most magnificent representation of the twenty-four-hour cycle. It rises through the formal Grove of Apollo into the Temple of Apollo (*opposite*), covered in gold suns. The grove, which took twelve years to build from 1764, was designed by Pigage in a synthesis of Rococo and English landscape styles. Flanked by sphinxes, it leads to a rocky representation of Mount Parnassus, sacred to Apollo and the Muses. As at Stourhead (pp. 90–5), the climb to Apollo is steep, rather than directly up the slopes of Parnassus, the path veering to the right through dark caverns before emerging to join Apollo in a heavenly panoramic view around the garden. The gloriously gilded sun motifs that decorate the iron balustrading are rather more spectacular than the actual statue of Apollo. Unusually, he is holding the lyre with his left hand – is he viewing us from 'the other side'? A contemporary visitor, Wilhelm Heinse, described Apollo as having 'a miserable looking set of buttocks'. The Temple of

Above: The interior of the
Bathhouse
Below, left: The Temple of Mercury
Below, right: The Temple of Minerva
Opposite: The Mosque

Mercury (Dusk) naturally follows the day's sun of the Temple of Apollo, and here Mercury is lulling Argos into slumber and sunset (*see* Barwick Park, pp. 144–5). The Mosque (*right*), flanked by minarets and reflected in a large pool, completes the twenty-four-hour cycle with its star-encrusted cupola: mosque in name only, it is actually a fine example of exotic Baroque, an imaginative transfer of Islamic decorative architectural ideas.

From the palace, the central axis runs through the circular French parterre to the river gods Danube and Rhine and the main lake. At the centre of the parterre is Barthélemy Guibal's Fountain of Arion, who is playing a lyre sitting astride the dolphin that rescued him from the sea and carried him to safety (the alternative interpretation is that the dolphin represents Christ coming to save man). The Stag Fountain (p. 96) marks the end of the parterre and, although Diana is absent, the story is suggested of Actaeon who, seeing her bathing, was changed into a stag and devoured by his own dogs. The two great white stags – mirror images – spout water into a mirror pond, a traditional representation of a door between the physical and the metaphysical world. Humans cannot see a god and survive, so they must pass through from this world to the next. There is a clear vista that opens to the lake: statues of Earth and Fire to the left and Water and Air to the right and a central memorial stone. Throughout there is a reverence for antiquity and overwhelming parallels to the Masonic 'triad' of Wisdom, Strength and Beauty, their rituals and association with King Solomon's Temple.

Geometric at its core, the outer margins of this *jardin français* soften into the irregularity of a *jardin anglais* and sinuous lakes. It is between these two respectable covers that the racy pages of the majority of the follies offer exhilarating and daring symbols to the initiated and provide the uninitiated with a desire to learn more.

Schloss Sanssouci, Potsdam

The impression as you enter this vast park, west of central Potsdam in former East Germany, is more *sans pareil* (without compare) than *sans souci* (without a care). Grand, wonderful and otherworldly are words that could be used to describe its extent and embodiment of Baroque power. It was created over two centuries under

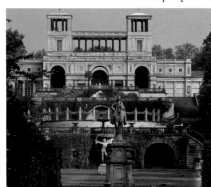

the influence of three powerful German rulers – Frederick the Great between 1744 and 1770, Frederick William IV 1826 to 1860 and finally Emperor William II from 1902 to 1913.

A grand central stone flight of steps cuts through six gently curving terraces up to Frederick the Great's palace (*left*), a stunning example of the classical virtues of beauty and utility. Frederick commanded that bowls brimming with grapes, peaches and figs should always be at his right hand. The terraces were constructed in heat-retaining brick containing 168 niches for figs, surrounded by wall-trained vines; in addition each terrace has twenty-eight glazed doors to ensure a propitious climate in winter. Espalier cherries, apricots and peaches were trained along the green trelliswork between the niches, the terraces culminating in clipped yew, potted citrus and pomegranates. The central rotunda of the palace celebrates the pleasures of the vines as bacchanalian figures, entwined with vines and grapes, besport themselves around the façade (*opposite*).

Above: Statues of Frederick the Great and Mercury on the Jubilee Terrace
Opposite: Bacchanalian figures celebrate the pleasures of the vine
Overleaf: A detail from the Chinese Tea House by Johann G. Büring

It was within this palace and its landscaped park that Frederick lived *sans souci*. Walking, or probably riding, west from the palace and terraces the park was planted into *bosquets* with diagonal rides to the river, the Sicilian Garden, the parterres, the Neues Palais and the Chinese Tea House (p. 104, *below, right*). Johann Gottfried Büring designed and built the Chinese Tea House set in its own gardens for Frederick between 1754 and 1757. The life-size gilded oriental figures inside and out (*overleaf*) are more Rococo-meets-chinoiserie than Baroque. The interior is gloriously gilded providing an oriental tableau set among golden palms – the details of the hair, costumes and decorum have a sense of Chinese opera. Although the naturalistic style of the *jardin anglo-chinois* had not reached Potsdam, the use of Chinese architectural detail such as that found in the Tea House and pagodas had. According to Chinese legend the upward-turning curves on pagodas were designed to impale dragons as they slid down the roof to attack. Appropriately the later Dragon House, built in the 1770s, is in the shape of a pagoda and now serves as a café; to date there have been no reports of attacks from dragons.

A Grand Tour of Italy was inspirational for the young Frederick William, as can be seen in the magnificent Orangery whose niches and roof balustrades are filled with classical allegorical figures, such as the Dancing Faun in mid-step as he accompanies himself with cymbals (p. 105). Tubs of oranges, palms and bays are still arranged along the upper terrace. In imperial

Above, left: The Dragon House

Above, right: The Neptune Temple

Below, left: The Roman Baths

Below, right: The Chinese
Tea House

Opposite: A dancing faun in an
alcove by the Orangery

Roman style there are garlands of fresh flowers between terms on the middle terrace both looking out across the estate and framing the view from the park. In 1913 Emperor William II built the stately Jubilee Terrace on which ornate parterres were planted; these have long gone but the equestrian statue of Frederick the Great rides on. Mercury wields a bow and arrow directed back to the palace of Sanssouci.

Near the Dragon House is the 'Spielfestung' – a grandiose toy fort fitted with miniature Krupp cannons built for the sons of William II. An idea enjoyed by his uncles at their summer home of Osborne House on the Isle of Wight built for them by their parents Queen Victoria and Prince Albert.

The majesty of the palace designed by Georg Wenzelaus von Knobelsdorff is matched by its surroundings: to the east is the Picture Gallery with Dutch Garden laid out in terrace beds on an axis with a fountain from which formal avenues radiate. Neptune's Grotto designed by Knobelsdorff 1751–7 is adjacent, set back in sylvan shade; a walk into the light leads to the cross-axis of the Hauptallee. The gently formal rhythms of the garden are ordered into military precision along the 2km/1¼ mile Hauptallee: starting at Knobelsdorff's Obelisk Portal raised in 1748, it links the gardens of the east with those of the west. En route to north and south are the elegant Orangery and Chinese buildings. The formal design and subtropical planting of the Sicilian Garden is a floriferous version of the Baroque enclosures of Villa Torrigiani (pp. 40–5). It contrasts with the hardy dark greens of the conifers, ivies and ferns that fill the cool, green Nordic Garden. The Baroque Neues Palais lies at the westernmost point – an architectural celebration of Prussian success in the Seven Years' War (*see* Wentworth Woodhouse, pp. 80–3). The palaces and gardens were built in architectural harmony rather than symmetry, enlivened by exuberant statues and carefree follies.

Larchill, Kilcock

Larchill in County Meath, 32km/20 miles from Dublin, is a modest-sized estate with an abundance of follies that punctuate a circular walk around the lake. The identity of their creator, however, remains a mystery. Of the ten follies at Larchill, several contribute to the debate on the definition of a folly. If one possible origin of the word folly is a corruption of the French *feuillée*, a word that is also adopted to describe a leafy (woody) setting, then such is the tight stand of mature beeches that adorn a spiral mound at Larchill. The first 'true' eighteenth-century folly is said to have been the great wall and quasi-military towers at Castle Howard designed by John Vanbrugh, and Larchill's Gibraltar (*overleaf*) is in a similar vein. A copy of a fortress on the Rock of Gibraltar, it is a miniature five-tower battlemented fort, reminiscent of that at Sanssouci (pp. 100–5) where mock naval battles were fought across the lake in the eighteenth century. There are several fine surviving examples of wall and tower follies in Ireland. The mossy follies at Larchill include a tower, wall, ornamental dairy, turf-roofed boathouse, gazebos and, on islands on a lake, Gibraltar – and a primitive circular temple.

The circular and battlemented Cockleshell Tower (*right*) at Larchill adorns the corner of two ends of the decorative garden wall. It provides a focal point for the enclosed garden and a splendid belvedere, its flat roof reached by an exterior staircase on the rear wall. The architecture gives the impression that there are three storeys, although the third is only implied by the detail of Gothic niches, string courses and windows. A door

at the base gives access to the ground- floor chamber, a simple domed room with deep Gothic latticed windows with some panes of coloured glass. The walls were originally painted ochre and blue (sand and sea) and coated in elaborate shell-work and the floor was finely patterned. Local shells such as cockles, mussels, limpets and razors were carefully arranged into patterns filled by tiny periwinkle shells. A cool retreat in summer but, if too chilly, provided with a fireplace to ensure every comfort. A narrow spiral staircase hugging the wall (*opposite*) leads to the first-floor chamber. The walls here are also decorated in fine shell-work, a large centrally placed conch in the apex of the domed ceiling providing a crowning note.

Along the garden wall there are widely spaced, ornate, double-stepped battlements which are capped with stone hemispheres. In the shelter of the wall an ornamental dairy was constructed with solid columns supporting Norman arches.

The other follies are encountered in the landscape around the lake. The gazebo seat is set in a wall at the bottom of a sloping plain on the opposite site of the lake from the house; the construction is classic in conception but crude in realisation, using rubble for the columns and walls including capping the piers with rubble domes. The hexagonal temple has three

Above: The Cockleshell Tower

Opposite: Cockleshell decoration on the staircase in the tower

Overleaf: The two island forts, known as Gibraltar and Spain

Above, left: A stained glass window
in The Cockleshell Tower
Above, right: The Gazebo Seat
Below, left: The Foxes' Earth
Below, right: The *ferme ornée*
Opposite: The Foxes' Earth with
a llama and an emu

supporting columns that form the front and three built
into the wall. There are three seats from which to enjoy
the panorama across the lake to the house and islands.
One seat is under the dome and the other two are
symmetrically placed against the walls on each side and
could have doubled as mounting blocks. The other
primitive gazebo is crudely rendered but situated on
high ground at the corner of a vast field sloping down
to the lake. It consists of four rough masonry columns
which are built into a boundary wall over which there is
a crude stone roof. This would have offered basic
shelter for hunt followers and surveyors of the follies.

By the late eighteenth century the term *ferme ornée*
was used to describe ornamental farm buildings rather
than bucolic farms with pretty hedges and walks. The
shelter for horses took the form of a range of Gothick
stables with fine stone dressings above the doors. Robert
Watson was Master of the West Meath Hounds and the
legend has grown that these follies were quarried from
his fertile mind. The story goes that Watson was a
passionate huntsman who desired to create his own
mausoleum as a climax to his follies. In a delightful
illusion of pure fantasy he built a rustic mausoleum that
could double as a foxes' earth – he believed he might be
reincarnated as a fox. Today it is grazed by rare breeds
and birds. It takes the form of a rectangular chamber
built into an artificial mound topped by a classically
designed but rustically conceived temple that is very
similar to the gazebo. The opening where a thick slice
has been taken out of the mound is marked by stout
stone piers and a low wall; flat ground then leads up to a
demi-lune façade edged in brick. The façade has a classic
but fairy-tale appearance with two arched windows
flanking a Gothic door. Too grand to safeguard a fox,
however, tucked away at ground level are two small
square openings tailored to vulpine dimensions. With
or without Watson, the pleasures of hunting
indubitably shaped these follies.

Reggia di Caserta, Caserta

North of Naples the flat plain of Caserta, safe from the ravages of war, was chosen to be the new capital of the Kingdom of Naples and Sicily by the Bourbon King Charles III. Ludwig Van Wittel known as Luigi Vanvitelli masterminded the designs of a palace to rival Versailles, with good town planning and magnificent hydraulic engineering, all oozing Baroque power over nature. An architect, landscape gardener and engineer Vanvitelli worked on the construction for twenty-two years until his death at Caserta in 1773. Unlike the king's father Philip V's palace at La Granja (pp. 76–9), the record-breaking cascade and canal lined up with the central axis of the palace.

Construction started with pomp and ceremony when the first stone was laid on 20 January 1752, and continued after the Bourbons had fled to Sicily and the kingdom was presented by Napoleon to Joseph Bonaparte. As at Versailles, water is used to dominate the 120ha/300 acre landscape, the grandeur of the palace reaching out some 3km/2 miles along a series of powerfully executed classical fountain scenarios to the Grande Cascata, a 78m/200ft cascade. Hydraulic power extended beyond the garden boundaries, and Vanvitelli and his son Carlo drilled through five mountains and built three viaducts to transport water from the Fizzo and Bronzo springs along a 40km/30 mile aqueduct to the Cascata.

Classical associations with water from the mythological lives of Diana and Actaeon, Venus and Adonis, and Ceres and Aeolus are played out in heroic scenes. They punctuate the Cascata from the rugged hillside to the ordered symmetry of the palace parterres. In the Fontana di Venere e Adone (*opposite*), Venus, the goddess of love and all growing things who is usually cast emerging serenely from the foam in a gently erotic form, is pleading with her young lover Adonis in a desperate attempt to dissuade him from hunting, her passions visibly aroused. Amorini play with his hunting dogs whilst the wild boar that will give him the mortal bite snarls in anticipation. The water moves relentlessly onwards down a series of twelve water steps.

In the Fontana di Cerere, Ceres holds up Trinacria, the medallion of Sicily. This is flanked by the Sicilian rivers of Anapo and Lineto, symbolic of the water needed by both kingdoms to ensure a successful harvest. As the waters descend the stories are framed in increasingly architectural settings: a series of symmetrical arches topped with shell motifs curve behind the mossy rocks of the Fontana di Eolo.

Above: Pan ready to pipe in the dawn

Opposite: The deadly wild boar awaits

Visitors can lean on the curving balustrade, decorated with statues struggling against stiff breezes and snake-encircled urns, to look down on the Aeolian scene. The combination of the turbulence from the waterfall and the puffed cheeks of the wind gods makes you want to turn up your collar against these mythological gales.

Nearest to nature, immediately below the turbulent genesis of the Grande Cascata, buttocks are hastily covered and Diana's bathing form modestly wrapped as the nymphs awaken to Actaeon's peeping. His punishment is swift, his head already metamorphosed into that of a stag as baying hounds turn to kill their prey (*above, left*). The portrayal of the dogs varies from distinctly lion-like, to mastiff and pointer. Do the heavy collars emphasise the fact that they have been let off the leash?

A lozenge of lawn separates all these breezes from

the canal that finishes the scheme: at one end is the
Dolphin Fountain (also known as the Fontana del
Canalone) complete with a central dolphin whose fins
are replaced with talons; nearest the palace is the
Hercules Bridge – definitely a place to lean and
survey other people's labours.

Many follies never make it further than grand
schemes and Caserta is no exception – Vanvitelli
planned to channel the cascade under the palace into
two canals that would flank the Via Appia along a
further 30km/18 miles to Naples.

In fact Caserta is a fine example of the folly of
choosing to prolong the swaggering Baroque style in
the exaggerated decadence of its vast elements. The
naturalistic setting of La Granja (pp. 64–7) and the
consummate movement of its sculptural groups quietly
outmanoeuvres the brash waterworks and stiff statues
of Caserta.

Above, left and right: Diana
punishes Actaeon for
peeping
Far, left: Detail of the
Dolphin Fountain
Left: Two figures holding a
basket on the perimeter
of the Fontana di Eolo
(Fountain of Aeolus)

Belvedere House, Mullingar

With a length of 55m/180ft, the Jealous Wall (*opposite*) in the grounds of Belvedere House is the largest sham wall in Ireland. It was constructed in 1760 for Robert Rochfort, Baron Bellfield, later 1st Earl of Belvedere, on his estate in County Westmeath. It dwarfs the Cockleshell Tower and wall at Larchill (pp. 106–11), being more on the scale of a large medieval castle, and has a glowering presence running across the landscape.

Above: The Rustic Arch
Opposite: The Jealous Wall

If 'Hell hath no fury like a woman scorned', the Jealous Wall has to be the monumental male equivalent. The marriage between Rochfort, one of the richest young men in Ireland, and Mary, daughter of the 3rd Viscount Molesworth, took place in 1736 and the couple lived in the family seat, Gaulston House. Robert, however, was an absentee husband, and Mary, lonely with young children, was befriended by Robert's young brother, Arthur, who lived nearby at Bellfield House. In 1743 Robert accused Mary of infidelity with Arthur and was supported by his other brother, George. Robert left his wife at Gaulston and moved to his newly completed Palladian villa, Belvedere House, some 8km/5 miles away, near the shores of Lough Ennell. Arthur was bankrupted and for thirty years Mary was incarcerated at Gaulston, with only servants to keep her company.

Robert had commissioned the architect Richard Castle to design Belvedere House, but the hot-headed baron soon quarrelled with his brother George, who commissioned Castle to build the larger Rochfort House (later known as Tudenham). Robert retaliated by blocking George's view with an enormous sham Gothick ruin, which because of Robert's cruel treatment of his wife, became known as the 'Jealous Wall'. Its design is attributed to a Florentine architect called Barradotte. The central flat façade is terminated by a seemingly circular tower, which neatly curves out of sight but is merely a half circle. The alternating straight, angled and curved lines of the ground plan ensure stability while providing the illusion of an imposing complex.

Belvedere House is set in beautiful parkland adorned with follies, including the Rustic Arch (*left*) which, with its exuberant grotesque stonework, looks more like a gate into a folkloric town. The designer was Thomas Wright of Durham, a mystic and philosopher. It may seem a contradiction in terms to class such a folly as a serious work of architecture, but he did apply a wealth of compositional and stylistic considerations to it. The exterior is a fusion of medieval and neoclassical designs: the Norman arched doorway, arrow slits and Gothic pointed windows suggest medieval origins, whereas the oriel window awaits the presence of a Venetian *bella donna* luring suitors. Wright illustrated it as a 'Gothic' arch in Plate M of 'Six Original Designs for Grottos' in his *Universal Architecture*.

Robert Rochfort rose through the social ranks to become Earl of Belvedere in 1756 and Master General of the Irish army in 1764. A later owner, Lt. Colonel Charles Howard-Bury, was the leader of the first attempt to climb Mount Everest in 1921.

The Pineapple, Dunmore House, Airth

The Dunmore Pineapple is reputed to be the most eccentric building in Scotland. Reaching 11m/37ft high, the beautifully proportioned stone pineapple was built in 1771 by John Murray, the 4th Earl of Dunmore, to mark his permanent return home to Airth near Falkirk from duties as the last British Governor of Virginia. It crowns a pavilion, probably designed by Robert Mylne, which was made ten years earlier as a summerhouse for the earls' 2.5ha/6 acre south-facing garden.

The entrances to the original pavilion were retained when the pineapple was added, as were the double construction walls that circulated warm air. On the north side steps lead up to a Gothic door – a subtle reminder of the native Scottish clime? – and the Gothic detail is echoed in the sash windows on each of the eight sides of the octagonal fruit. A classical columned loggia frames the south entrance in an echo of Italian gardens. The walls flanking the south entrance were formerly covered in glass panels so that, as at Sanssouci, (pp. 100–5) tender fruits could be ripened. Gardeners were housed in bothies on either side.

A preserve of the rich, growing pineapples was a skilled exercise for trained gardeners, and this folly is a macrocosm of that cultural care. Exquisite in detail, the stiff serrated edges of the lowest and topmost leaves and the plump berry-like fruits are all cunningly graded so that water cannot accumulate anywhere, ensuring that frozen trapped water cannot damage the delicate stonework. Sadly the identity of the designer is unknown, although some have attributed it to the Scottish architect Sir William Chambers, who is known to have produced a number of outstanding buildings in Kew Gardens.

In the eighteenth century, American sailors would traditionally bring home pineapples to put on their gateposts to publicise their homecoming and to serve as a welcome to visitors, as can be seen at Colonial Williamsburg. Pineapples were adopted as the symbol of hospitality throughout the American colonies. This is classic food for thought – anything the Americans could do Dunmore could do better? In his *Gardener's Dictionary* of 1746, Philip Miller, 'Gardener to the Worshipful Company of Apothecaries at their Botanic Garden in Chelsea', describes five species of 'Pine-apple' (*Ananas*) over ten pages. He recommends the finest as the Pyramidal Pineapple with a yellow flesh that was not so astringent and could be eaten in great quantity. As a fellow Scot, he surely would have delighted in this jumbo pineapple that almost rivals the pyramids of Egypt.

Above: The north façade
Opposite: The south façade with evidence of the former glasshouses

Désert de Retz, Chambourcy

West of Paris and on the edge of the Forest of Marly, near Chambourcy, lies a picturesque landscape decorated with an array of *fabriques* or follies laden with cryptic symbolism. The inventive mind behind these intriguing structures was François-Nicolas Henri Racine du Jonquoy, known as M. de Monville. He bought the derelict estate in 1774 and, up until the French Revolution in 1789, engaged the architect François Barbier to create his *désert* – a fashionable French retreat where one could entertain one's friends without troubling about convention, either social and moral.

Far from the controlling Baroque formalities of André le Nôtre, the Désert de Retz is a celebration of Jean-Jacques Rousseau's untamed nature and bucolic productivity – a *jardin anglais* and *ferme ornée*. The exercise had already been undertaken by the Marquis de Girardin at Ermenonville, where serendipitously Rousseau had died, and also by the Duc de Chartres at Parc Monceau. Now Monville, an unconventional dilettante who, among his multiple skills, was considered the best archer in Europe and boasted a steel and black velvet bow, undertook the recreation of a landscape bristling with artificial ruins that would suggest an inherited past.

The original (no longer extant) entrance from the royal forest of Marly took visitors into the womb-like darkness of a grotto. With echoes of the Château de la Bastie (pp. 18–21), it provided a ritualistic (Masonic) sense of being born into another world, the visitor emerging as both spectator and actor. The torch-bearing satyrs flanking the jagged rocks that formed the entrance to the grotto were probably inspired by Vitruvius' recommendation that satyrs should be placed in landscapes 'ornamented with trees, caves, hills and of rural objects in imitation of nature'. Safely delivered from the sacred passage, a winding path led the visitor past an Egyptian pyramid disguising an ice house (p. 122, *right*). Its central door opens into an underground chamber and the outer steps lead to a shallow platform running round the sides (*see* the Château de Groussay, pp. 198–203).

Whereas the English gardens of Stourhead (pp. 90–5) and Stowe (pp. 64–9) were designed to evoke qualities of calmness, smoothness and clarity, Monville's purpose was, in much the same manner as a Salvator Rosa painting, to strike awe, fear and terror in the eye of the beholder. His gigantic Column House was a folly-like echo of Piranesi's engravings of classical views. It was built in 1780 in the form of the quintessential emblem of classical antiquity and a significant Masonic symbol – the broken fluted column. Some 15m/50ft in diameter, it contained his main residence and was articulated with rectangular, square and oval openings to the four floors within, while the 'decaying' upper parts were conveniently fractured to allow light into the attic rooms. Monville lived here surrounded by interiors that were gloriously neoclassical: oval rooms containing

Above: The circular staircase in the Column House
Opposite page: The Column House or Broken Column

rare plants, marble fireplaces, paintings and busts of Benjamin Franklin and George Washington – both of whom were Freemasons. The rooms were lined with mirrors to reflect the ornamentation within and nature without, and the shafts of light that filled the central spiral staircase (p. 121) enabled him to place there a faïence vase planted with exotics such as Farnese acacias, currants from Buenos Aires and jasmines from the Azores. He also had a laboratory for his alchemical experiments. The concept of ovals within a circular column is said to be the inspiration for Jefferson's Rotunda Library at the University of Virginia.

A contemporary visitor, the Prince de Ligne, questioned whether the great height of the Column House symbolised the wrath of God upon his children and its resemblance to the Tower of Babel. The name of the Belgian Prince Charles-Joseph de Ligne interestingly weaves through this and similar gardens; he was a great admirer of both Rousseau and Voltaire. He wrote a commentary on European gardens in 1781, advised Monville, Marie-Antoinette, the Duc de Chartres and laid out the *jardin anglais* at Beloeil in Belgium.

Beyond the Column House there was an open-air theatre and winding paths led to other follies, such as the Temple of Repose and the Temple of Pan. Then, serving both practical and picturesque purposes, the Turkish (*opposite, above*) and Tartar tents. Monville's first residence, the 'Chinese House' by the lake, collapsed in

1967 but was well recorded in contemporary drawings. It was built of teak on a stone base from which a spring flowed, feeding a brook that tumbled into the lake with two small islands. The exterior resembled bamboo with geometrical panels painted red and violet and, like the Pagode de Chanteloup (pp. 124–5), with cartouches containing Chinese ideograms.

Such was the allure of this awesome dramatic landscape, described as a Masonic theatre, namely visuals without rituals, that it attracted an esoteric visitor list – contemporaries such as Marie-Antoinette when she was planning the Petit Hameau at Versailles, Thomas Jefferson, the amateur alchemist King Gustavus III of Sweden and Philippe Égalité (the Duc d'Orléans and one time Masonic Grand Master of the Grand Orient) plus, nearly two hundred years later, the writer Colette and the Surrealists Hans Arp and André Breton.

The original life of the Désert de Retz was brief, and as with Sleeping Beauty the brambles sealed its fate and it was left to gently disintegrate. It took nearly two hundred years for a saviour to arrive in the form of Olivier Choppin de Janvry, who bought the estate in 1984 with Jean Marc Heffler. They meticulously restored the surviving *fabriques* and picturesque passages of the park. The painstaking restoration included diligently replicating the cracks and widening chinks that let light into the 'Broken Column'. Restored but closed to the public it remains awesome.

Pagode de Chanteloup, Amboise

A poignant monument to lost grandeur, the Pagode de Chanteloup, rising gracefully through seven storeys to 44m/144ft, is all that remains of the fabulous park that the Grand Minister to Louis XV, the Duc de Choiseul, created on the margins of the forest of Amboise from 1761.

Like the châteaux and buildings of the Loire region, the pagoda (built in 1775 and restored in 1910 by the architect René Edouard André) was constructed using the local tufa, which is soft to quarry and cut but which hardens on contact with the air, the resultant caves being ideal for wine storage and growing mushrooms. The fine creamy-white stone is carved with acanthus and pineapples, and decorated with Chinese ideograms symbolising love, wisdom and friendship. The design, attributed to Louis-Denis Le Camus, is a grand neo-classical Greek Revival interpretation of the Chinese, as can be seen especially well on the interior spiral staircase (*left*). Rather than the hallmark overhanging roof and upturned curves of Sanssouci (*see* pp. 100–5),

the ground floor is a peristyle formed around sixteen Doric columns echoing the portal of the former Château de Chanteloup. Seven storeys rise in a diminishing cone, four of the levels with delicately wrought iron balconies, three in *chinois* style, the topmost more robust and plain. There are references to marble plaques on the walls of the elegant first-floor room celebrating Choiseul's faithful friends. The final note is Chinese – the golden ball on the pinnacle of the roof.

The pagoda is reflected in the surviving *demi-lune* lake from which radiated seven or eight magnificent lime and elm avenues. Climb the narrow spiral staircase for majestic views to the town of Amboise and across its forest and the fertile Loire Valley, which in the eighteenth century also provided a viewing point for the hunts. From 1802 the owner count J.-A. Chaptal used the estate for the experimental growing and processing of sugar beet – the roots of the French sugar industry. The Duc de Choiseul's extravagant wedding cake now formed the centrepiece to a sweet landscape.

Often implicit in the term 'folly' is that the cost is immaterial – even Choiseul was forced to contemplate his folly when the final pagoda cost 40,000 écus rather than the expected 8,000 and he was forced to sell in 1823. The new owners proceeded to demolish most of the buildings on the estate, leaving no trace of the castle that had dazzled contemporaries, and so that all that remains today are the Pagoda and the lake.

Mussenden Temple, Derry

Near Downhill in County Derry, where the cliffs rise 60m/200ft from the Atlantic Ocean, stands Mussenden Temple, poised elegantly above the awful and sublime beating of the seas below. The beauty for whom it was named, Frideswide Mussenden née Bruce, enjoyed an affectionate chaste relationship with her older distant cousin, Frederick Hervey, the Marquis of Bristol and Bishop of Derry, until she died at the age of twenty-two.

What better description for a folly builder than: '... the infamous Earl Bishop, Frederick Hervey ... refined, well-travelled, and enthusiastic patron of the arts enjoyed great wealth but little common sense'. Alexander Pope had counselled Lord Burlington, much of whose wealth also derived from Ireland, to 'consult the genius of the place in all; that tells the waters or to rise, or fall ...' and then advised the creation of order out of chaos. The chaotic, rhythmic lashings of the sea without provide a wild contrasting genius to the created order of the library within, where Hervey housed his magnificent book collection. In ferocious weather servants called to wait on their master had to crawl to and from the main house. Echoing its rugged surroundings the classical Greek sandstone temple, said to have been inspired by the Temple of Vesta at Tivoli, is built on a rough basalt stone plinth. The sixteen columns and the entablature are of the Corinthian order whose acanthus-leafed capitals symbolise feminine virtue and beauty. At his ancestral Ickworth in Suffolk Hervey built a grand house with duplicate central rotunda which his wife referred to as 'a stupendous monument of folly'.

Despite being a Protestant bishop Hervey demonstrated a liberal attitude by building a Catholic chapel for his workmen in the crypt. Such were his Papist sympathies in fact that Horace Walpole waspishly observed that he qualified for a cardinal's hat. One wonders if he actually disliked his Anglican priests. In 1784 he organised summer horse races between his rotund clergymen and the slimline Presbyterian ministers. Apparently the bishop 'laughed heartily at the discomfort of the church' as the ministers were consistently first past the post whilst the vicars fell off their mounts. He then selected a strip of quicksand for a running race between the county's fattest clergy, the prize being the most valuable stipend; he watched delightedly from his temple vantage point as they flailed and sank.

There is no longer anything to read within, but there are friezes, finely carved mouldings and an inscription in Latin from Lucretius' *De Rerum Natura* (On the Nature of Things) decorating the exterior. The Latin inscription 'SUAVE MARI MAGNO TURBANTIBUS AEQUORA VENTIS, E TERRA MAGNUM ALTERIUS SPECTARE LABOREM' translates as: 'When the winds are throwing the seas into confusion in the great ocean, it is sweet to watch from land the great hardship of others'. In more classical metre, Dryden rendered it as:

Tis pleasant safely to behold from shore
The rolling ship and hear the tempest roar

Above: The Temple overlooking the Atlantic Ocean
Opposite: The approach to the Temple

De Notelaer, Bornem

Above Antwerp the riverscape is gentler around De Notelaer or Le Notaire or near Hingene, which has been described as a beautiful fusion of nature and culture designed by Charles de Wailly (1730-98). The building is a northern European interpretation of Baroque style, especially the sash and round windows that lie within the grand arches of vermiculated stone on the northern façade. The top of the dome that peeps above this seeming *villa rustica* hints at the grand southern façade that exudes a sense of Italy and the Veneto. The rough-hewn local stone is arched and filled with brickwork, from which arises finely detailed masoned stone and balustrading. The balustrade around the top of the dome means that visitors can enjoy extensive vistas across the flat countryside and the waters of the river and ornamental canal. The lower half of the house is literally behind the protective dyke but the first-floor windows overlook it.

Above: The domed Belvedere
Opposite: The north façade
Overleaf: The Italian Saloon

The octagonal structure is emphasised by outer columns that support a covered walk between them and the glazed doors. Above the windows four classical river gods represent the local River Schelde, which rises in France, and its tributaries the Leie, Dender and Durme; the gods lie at ease gently pouring water, the symbol of life, onto the scene. With the proximity of the dyke, the area is in constant danger of flooding so these are gods to be respected.

The domed octagonal room is known as the Italian Saloon, and the exquisite decoration of its ceiling was inspired by the frescoes at Herculaneum and Pompeii. It is supported by eight marble columns, and above each door the four elements are portrayed as deities in imitation bronze: Jupiter, Neptune wielding his triton and driving his hippocamps (horses with shells for hooves) through the waters, and Cybele and Apollo riding the chariot of dawn; each god divided by a panel of two basilisks. Between them are blue background cartouches of gods such as Venus and Cupid. Higher still a frieze of classical putti and arabesques dance around, above that the repeating design of gilded flower and acanthus leaf.

The centre of the dome is glazed so that blue or stormy skies, or twinkling stars, are framed by the thirty-one alternating decorative panels of the inner dome. A series of arabesques forms a lively chain of classical incident: first either acanthus leaves evolving into a nymph supporting cherries or sphinxes supporting cereal crops; then a cartouche of one of the Muses, or a rather glum nymph, and below them an arbutus garland and lyre. The arbutus (or strawberry tree) was a popular plant in Roman frescoes because it is evergreen and flowers and fruits simultaneously. The chain is completed by a rabbit or a multi-rayed sun. Equally dazzling as the dome above is the chevron- and diamond-patterned parquet floor beneath your feet.

What enlightened folly to give riparian rights alongside reeds, rushes and warblers to a light-filled dome of palazzo proportions.

ROMANTICISM & INNOVATION

Beauty, in the nineteenth century, was now firmly in the eye of the beholder, and symbolism related to personal experience rather than being a programmed response to classically appointed emotions. The design objectives, *Firmitas*, *utilitas* and *venustas*, as outlined by Vitruvius in his *Ten Books of Architecture* (*c.* 27BC), which had shaped the Villa d'Este and the Désert de Retz, can be applied to an extraordinarily innovative period when even the most extravagant buildings followed his principles.

Firmitas underpins the structures in the sense of durability and strength, assets harnessed by innovative technology. *Utilitas*, meaning commodity, utility and convenience, became the byword for the Arts and Crafts movement. *Venustas* stems from Venus, the goddess of love, whose statues and temples expressing her virtues of grace, charm, beauty and loveliness equate most closely with romantic follies.

Brightling Park, Brightling

In the opening years of the nineteenth century the squire of Brightling Park in East Sussex was entertaining guests in London and offered a wager that the spire of Dallington church was visible from his country house. Squire Jack Fuller was mistaken: a small ridge obscured the view. Unable to move the obstruction, he constructed a sham spire near Woods Corner so as not to lose his winnings. This elegant cone with the nickname of 'Sugar Loaf' (*right*), rising to 12m/40ft, was erected to be visible from the dining room of Brightling Park. It has a smoothness that matches the contemporary blocks of sugar that were delivered to households.

Life was sweet for Jack Fuller who reputedly weighed more than twenty stone (280lb or 127kg) and was larger than life in every sense; he had inherited a fortune at the age of twenty from his uncle and owned vast tracts of land which included extensive sugar plantations in Jamaica. He was a Member of Parliament, philanthropist and a generous patron of the arts, buying many paintings from J.M.W. Turner; his sister Rose married Lancelot 'Capability' Brown's son Lancelot and he consulted the architect Humphry Repton.

As well as the Sugar Loaf, Fuller created an obelisk and other garden buildings at Brightling. In 1803 he built his first folly a summerhouse in Coade stone manufactured in Lambeth and in 1805 he commissioned Sir Robert Smirke to design a small 'temple' rotunda, Smirke also designed the observatory, complete with a Camera Obscura. This observatory was not only built for star-gazing but so that his servants could herald his return from London, thus ensuring that all was

prepared and ready in the big house on his arrival. Fuller also had a hermit's tower built hoping that a needy body would simply arrive and take up residence – but it never happened.

In 1811, twenty-three years before his death, Fuller built his own tomb (*opposite*), a pyramid which stands 7.6m/25ft high in the churchyard of St Thomas à Becket, Brightling.

According to local legend Fuller was entombed in the pyramid in full dress and top hat seated at a table set with a roast chicken and a bottle of wine. During renovations in the 1980s it was discovered that Fuller is buried in the conventional manner beneath the pyramid.

The ninth verse of Grey's *Elegy* is inscribed on one wall:

Above: The Sugar Loaf

Opposite: Pyramid tomb of 'Mad' Jack Fuller

> *The boast of heraldry, the pomp of power;*
> *And all that beauty, all that wealth e'er gave,*
> *Awaits alike th' inevitable hour:-*
> *The paths of glory lead but to the grave.*

After 1815, as elsewhere in England (*see* Stancombe Park p. 142–3) there was a high level of unemployment in the country and Fuller used the local unemployed to build a wall around his entire Rose Hill estate. Unlike Byron he was mad, good and safe to know.

The Royal Pavilion, Brighton

The folly of the Prince of Wales, later King George IV, is splendidly encapsulated in the Royal Pavilion at Brighton. The prince rebelled against the elegance of Regency architecture and, in a fantastic revolt against classicism, as Nigel Nicolson observed, 'the pleasure-domes of Xanadu were transported to an English seaside town'. Where pagodas and chinoiserie hinted at the delights of the Chinese Empire, oriental pavilions were an outward display of British imperialism and evoked the enchanted rule of sultans and maharajahs, resulting in an exotic style which made a brief but dazzling appearance. Only the green painted canopies over the balconies (*left*) provided the template for Regency villas across the Empire.

Above: The central dome of the Steine Front

Opposite: The mirrored chimney piece in the Music Room

Overleaf: Roofline from the west

The pavilion is an edifice of such unashamed extravagance – its lines being rather more elegant than those of its creator – that songsters of jolly jingles noted the happy coincidence that 'pavilion' rhymes with 'million'. Contemporary comments considered it to be both folly and architectural extravaganza. The radical William Cobbett thought its domes were inspired by the Kremlin. The essayist William Hazlitt described them as a collection of stone pumpkins and pepper pots. According to the clergyman and wit Sidney Smith, 'The dome of St Paul's must have come down to Brighton and pupped.'

The prince had first visited Brighton on the Sussex coast in 1783, in search of a sea water cure for glandular swellings, a treatment popularised by the writings of Dr Richard Russell. Two years later, he returned with Mrs Fitzherbert, to whom he was secretly married, to live in a farmhouse in a prominent location on the main road to London and facing the Steine, a fashionable area on which to promenade. Henry Holland tripled the modest proportions of the farmhouse and added a rotunda to create a noble Palladian villa named 'The Marine Pavilion'.

A roll of Chinese wallpaper so entranced the prince that he created a Chinese gallery and chinoiserie spread throughout the pavilion; then the Chinese whim was overtaken by the discovery of the Indian Moorish style. In 1805 William Porden designed the Royal Riding House and Stables, inspired by the mosques and palaces of India. Then Humphry Repton was asked to prepare a 'Red Book' – his hallmark presentation of his report, notes and drawings, with before and after views, bound in red Moroccan leather. Repton observed that motifs in Gothic architecture corresponded to buds, in Grecian to acanthus leaves and that the new oriental influences were echoed in flowers such as water lilies or the lotus – the Bath stone Indian pillars have lotus bases. The roofs of the domes are enlivened with applied leaf patterns from the small overlapping leaves on the lower dome to the banana leaves that fall from the pinnacles.

However, Repton's former partner and rival, John Nash, was hired to 'quite eclipse Napoleon'. From 1815 to 1823 Nash used new technology to further enlarge the villa, superimposing the cast iron framework over

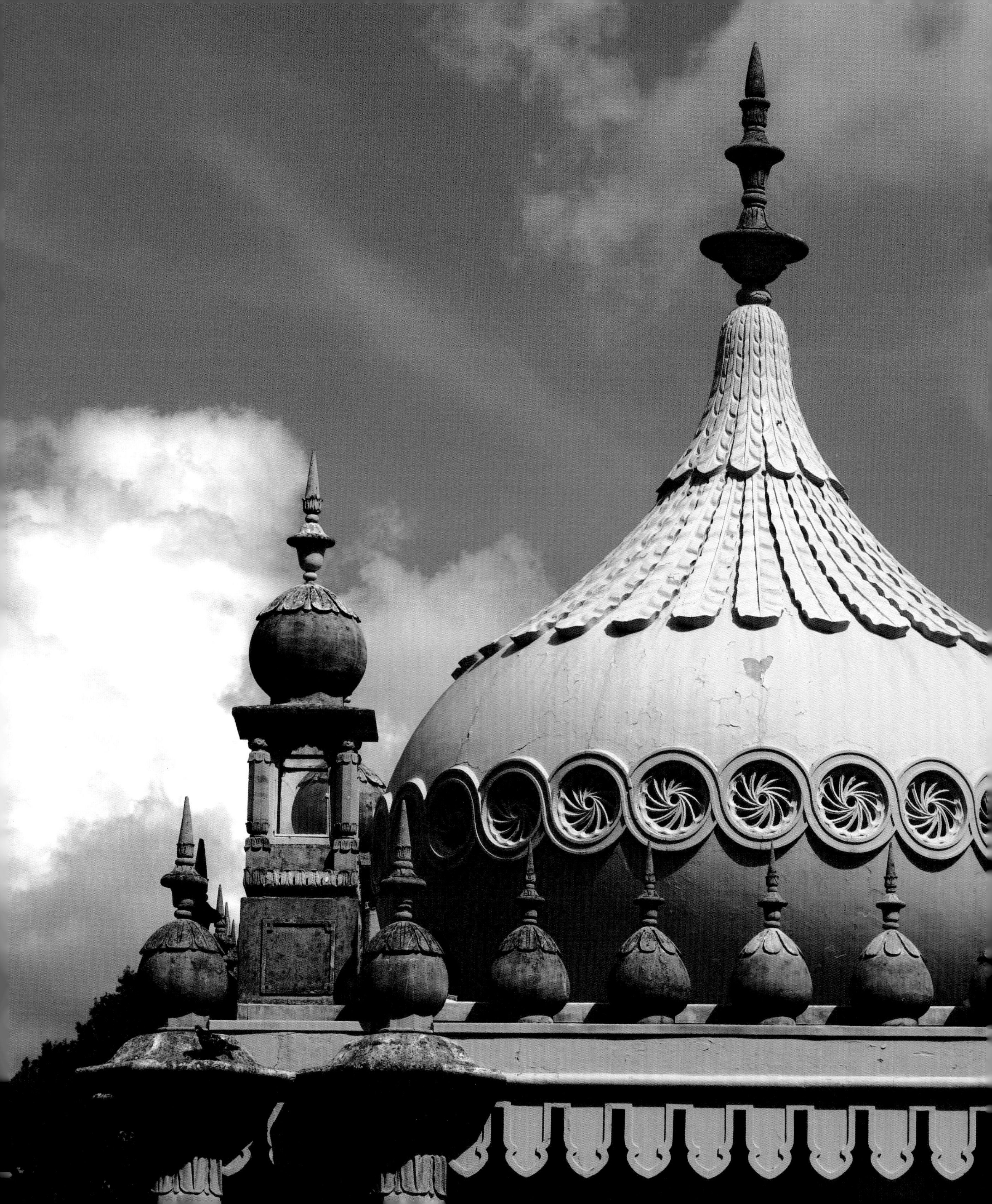

Above: The west front

Opposite: The Banqueting Room

Holland's Marine Pavilion which enabled him to add domes and minarets. He copied Repton's Indian style but incorporated more scenic effect by referring back to and reinterpreting Thomas and William Daniell's *Oriental Scenery*, published in 1795 and illustrated with Hindu and Islamic buildings seen during their travels.

Nash's roofline offered a harmonic rhythm (*previous page*). Of the two designs he submitted, the one with bulbous onion domes of authentic Indian shape was rejected, while the concave spires that could have adorned the tented pavilion of a Saracen warrior in one of Walter Scott's romantic novels was selected. The decorative stucco mouldings, architraves, friezes and cornices all romantically enhance the grand canvas effect of eclectically shaped domes, minarets and pepper-pot chimneys.

The Indian exteriors (*above*) and Chinese interiors were not viewed as a clash of cultures but as romantic concepts of the Orient. The interiors are gorgeously colourful, gilded and mirrored so the treasures, especially of the Banqueting (*opposite*) and Music

Rooms, are elegantly reflected. The stained glass in the round, tear-drop and diamond casements added a kaleidoscope of coloured light. Structurally the Saloon retains Holland's original plan but not the décor, such as the birds on the wallpaper which seem to flit across the delicately painted alcoves. There is an exotic feel to the Music Room – water-lily lights, a painted harp and brass-inlaid rosewood piano rest under a golden fish-scaled dome, and the walls are painted with Chinese landscapes in scarlet, yellow and gold lacquer (*see* Sanssouci, pp. 100–5). Gilded palm trunks support the mirrored glass, attacked by fearsome flying dragons, while snakes writhe in serpentine fashion around painted pillars.

The chandeliers in both the Music Room and Banqueting Room were among the first in the country to be converted to gas in 1818. In the latter a vast silver dragon hovers from a decorative palm tree in the dome, grasping a 9m/30ft chandelier in its claws. As the crystals of the chandelier fall, four gilded dragons rise up holding open lotus-shaped lamps (*opposite*).

Stancombe Park, Dursley

Below the curve of Stinchcombe Hill, Stancombe Park lies at the head of the valley midway between the Cotswold villages of Dursley and Wotton-under-Edge. The house is framed by classically patterned box-edged flower borders that echo the Roman mosaic floors that have been found on the site. Cows graze contentedly in the adjoining pasture around the first lake. Beyond, unseen, lies a folly garden rooted in Regency romance – the setting for a story about the Reverend David Edwards who, having married stout Miss Purnell for her money, sought passion in the arms of his gypsy lover.

Finding your way into this Regency Cretan labyrinth of follies is an exercise in romantic eccentricity. A walk lined with a topiary menagerie leads down past a stone font bubbling with spring water to the first tunnel which is guarded by Cerberus, the three-headed dog who guarded the underworld. Then you emerge briefly into the light for a vista of the lake, before returning to the dark, fossil- and shell-encrusted west tunnel. The Egyptian motifs (*right*) probably celebrate Nelson's victory on the Nile – apt as the landscaping work provided employment for soldiers returning from the Napoleonic Wars. Entry to the icehouse en route is through a whalebone arch, the jaw bone of a foolish whale that swam up the River Severn. One final tunnel and, like Augustin in *Le Grand Meaulnes*, you find yourself in 'The Lost Domain', an idealised walk with representations of Egyptian, Greek and Chinese civilisations. Local nineteenth-century legend whispers that the Reverend Edwards designed these tunnels so that his Junoesque wife could not squeeze through to track him down when he was dallying with his gypsy lover.

A wild boar on a small island surveys the classic Doric temple mirrored in the largest lake (*opposite*). Built on an eminence, not only is the architecture pure Greek but so is the planting around its foundations: an elegant interpretation of order arising from chaos. The temple was, and remains, decorated and furnished for a pair of lovers, with yellow marble Ionic columns leading through to an elegantly Italianate salon; the one bedroom has swagged curtains leading to the large double bed.

The 1940s brought two colourfully contrasting characters to Stancombe Park: Doris Hooper, who arranged bathing beauty contests on the jetty, and Evelyn Waugh who lived nearby and wrote passages of *Brideshead Revisited* that allude to Stancombe. The childhood imagination of our photographer Nic Barlow was nurtured by this folly-filled landscape. He grew up partying to vicar-and-gypsy and *Le Grand Meaulnes* themes and went on to chase follies around Europe until he caught them on film for further amusement.

Above: The Moorish Keyhole Arch with Egyptian glyph

Opposite: The Doric Temple

Barwick Park, Yeovil

Sound reason seems to have prompted George Messiter to build four follies in the grounds of Barwick Park just south of Yeovil, for they mark the boundaries of the park at the four cardinal points. Whether it is equally sound to consume treacle before running a marathon seems more questionable.

On the eastern boundary, the folly topped by fleet-footed Mercury celebrates speedy Jack who ran messages from Barwick Park to London sustained by nothing more than treacle, which is why it is commonly known as Jack the Treacle-Eater Tower (*opposite*). Mercury is recognisable by his winged hat and *talaria* (winged sandals) and by his *caduceus* (a rod entwined by two serpents, a symbol that is thought to have originated in Egypt). The *caduceus* was also a white wand carried by Roman heralds when they went to treat for peace, so in the hands of Mercury, the herald of the gods, it achieved peace by sending people to sleep (*see* Schwetzingen, pp. 96–9). Mercury acted as messenger to his godly parents Jupiter and Maia, and was the god of science, commerce and thieves. The Ham stone and ashlar circular tower atop a rubble-stone arch has a battlemented parapet and a conical stone roof that doubles as a home for other winged messengers – doves or pigeons. Although there is an open rough-stone staircase on one side of the arch leading to a wooden door in the tower, it seems unlikely that either the guano or the squabs were gathered, but the gentle cooing and patterns of flight would have been pleasing.

The northern boundary of Barwick Park is marked by the 15m/50ft high Fish Tower, so named because it formerly had a large golden weather vane in the shape of a fish inside an iron cage. The rough rock tower is punctuated by six evenly placed slit windows that light the interior. Evidence suggests that it originally had a spiral staircase so Messiter's guests could climb to the top. To the south the Obelisk or Needle (12m/40ft high) is without inscription and leans rather like the tower in Pisa. To the west Messiter's Cone (*left*), rising to 23m/75ft, is a tall, thin and hollow 'spire' that, with its symmetrical piercing, is reminiscent of Breton church spires, an architectural device that allows the wind to percolate through rather than buffet the structure. It stands on a squat cylinder standing on three arches crowned by a ball, and is also known as 'The Rose Tower'.

The exact dates of their construction are open to debate. Local legend recounts that during a time of depression in the 1820s the building of some if not all of these follies provided employment.

Above: Messiter's Cone
Opposite: Jack the Treacle-Eater Tower

Kasteel Rosendael, Rozendaal

Kasteel Rosendael in Rozendaal, Gelderlan, is an elegantly naturalistic nineteenth-century landscape that provides a setting for a profusion of seventeenth- and eighteenth-century Baroque shell-work. It has been described as a Dutch cross between the Villa d'Este (*see* pp. 28–33) and Rousham House in Oxfordshire. The use of the natural topography to create an open flowing valley was conceived in 1836 by A.L. Adolph Torck. The work was undertaken by the landscape gardener Jan David Zocher Jr, who also designed Holland's first public park.

During the late seventeenth century the medieval castle was owned by a confidant of William III, Jan van Arnhem, who commissioned some spectacular waterworks and water jokes from Daniel Marot, who had helped William and Mary create the interiors and gardens at Hampton Court Palace in England. In 1721 Arnhem's great-nephew Lubbert Adolf Torck inherited the estate; he modernised the castle and entrusted Marot with the task of designing follies between the two lakes divided by a crescent shaped shell wall. At this time Holland was the centre of the European trade in shells, and these follies are decorated with fifty different species of shell and six of coral. Torck was married to Petronella van Hoorn who was the daughter of the Governor of the Dutch East Indies and so a likely source for the shells. Between 1685 and 1692 the English physician Martin Lister had published the first reference book on shells, *Historia Conchyliorum*, and from the late seventeenth century shells were used artistically for festoons, pedestals, buffets, path and grottoes.

The Shell Wall (*opposite*) uses sound and movement to complement colour and pattern – a harmony repeated in all the follies. It is exuberantly decorated with shells, figures and fountains that provide classical references and the gnomon keeps track of the time. In contrast to the Rococo shell motif, the Baroque garden pavilion (*right*) was entered by two bright blue doors, the interior richly decorated in blue and gold and fitted with a washroom and alcove for a bed.

The Shell Gallery encompasses about 150sq.m/1614 sq.ft of grandiose architecturally conceived wall in a purple and white scheme which harks back to Versailles. The effect is achieved with the characteristically blue-grey Dutch stone and bands of white marble so often used by Marot that they are referred to as being Marotesque. There are alcoves with exquisite shell-work, chambers and an elegantly stepped cascade (*overleaf*).

In 1854 ownership passed to R.J.C. Baron van Pallandt, who introduced exotic trees. Today the follies have been restored in the romantic setting of the nineteenth-century park and you can sit at the end of the rainbow as the sun plays through the cascade.

Above: The Baroque garden pavilion
Opposite: The Shell Wall
Overleaf: The Shell Gallery Cascade

Palácio da Pena, Sintra

Mists shroud the Sintra Mountains north-west of Lisbon, and the moist microclimate away from the drying heats of the capital allows flowers, grasses and trees to flourish. Architecturally, culturally and horticulturally an eclectic band of invaders have left their mark here – the classic masonry of the Romans, the arabesques of the Moors and the Picturesque of the nineteenth-century English and German Romantics.

Above: The Moorish Kiosk
Opposite: The Duck Island
Overleaf: The palace

The Palácio da Pena, which sits on one of the highest peaks and dominates the Serra de Sintra landscape, is like a fairy-tale castle – a confection of pointed turrets, golden domes and crenellated walls (*overleaf*). This palatial summer residence was a romantic restoration designed by the German architect Baron Wilhelm Ludwig von Eschwege for Duke Ferdinand of Saxe-Coburg-Gotha-Koháry, a cousin of England's Prince Albert. Ferdinand had married Queen Maria II in 1836, becoming Dom Fernando II, and was greatly enamoured of Sintra and especially Pena, which at that time consisted of the deserted monastery of Nossa Senhora da Pena (Our Lady of Pena) and a Moorish castle surrounded by bare rocks. He bought the estate in 1838 and immediately started restoring it and planting an extensive forest. In 1840 he extended the road right up to the palace, and work on his 'Ideal Palace' continued until his death. He used the Meira brothers from Afife to create the interior stucco-work that constitutes a nineteenth-century fusion of Arab and Indian styles and is breathtaking in its delicacy. The result is one of the finest examples of Romantic architecture within a romantic park in Portugal.

The park extends to 200ha/500 acres, the forest below the Jardim das Camélias being planted with species of plants that represented all the countries and regions of the Portuguese Empire. Lake gardens were created that included such follies as a Gothic monk's grotto and an extensive medieval-style duck castle (*opposite*), complete with castellations and ramparts. On the crest of one of the lower mountains is the Castelo dos Mouros, the Moorish Castle, built in the eighth century and heavily restored by Fernando. A climb into its turrets gives a romantic view over the moss-covered granite boulders that cover much of the mountainside down to the old town of Sintra and up to the palace.

In addition to the Islamic details of Kufic script around the domes (*left*), the Moorish tradition of *azulejos* (tilework) abounds on the roofs and walls of the palace and its associated buildings. Like other kingly romantic follies in the nineteenth century, such as the Royal Pavilion at Brighton (pp. 136–41), and Schloss Linderhof in Ettal (pp. 164–7), the architectural extravaganzas of Pena have been suitably tailored to national characteristics.

Biddulph Grange, Biddulph

The Victorian world of gardens at Biddulph Grange in Staffordshire anticipated in miniature Prince Albert's 1851 Great Exhibition within the Crystal Palace. The magnificent features – both ornamental buildings and rockwork – that transport visitors from the heart of the English Potteries to Italy, China and Egypt by way of a Scottish glen, were dreamt up by three innovative Victorians. James Bateman, for whom Spode made a plate to commemorate his twenty-first birthday, was still only twenty-six in 1838 when he published the first of six parts of his *Orchidaceae of Mexico and Guatemala* – the largest botanical book ever produced. He also had a passion for ferns, which was shared by his wife Maria Egerton Warburton whose knowledgeable arrangement of herbaceous borders predates those of the great Gertrude Jekyll. Edward Cooke, a marine artist whose grotesque sketches could easily rival the monsters of the Villa Palagonia (pp. 70–5), completes this triumvirate. The landscape of dramatic scenes provided a stage for connoisseur plant collections from the four corners of the earth.

The Batemans' wealth derived from coal mines, ironworks and cotton mills, and in 1840 they bought Biddulph Grange. A contender for the most hideous house in Staffordshire, it was nonetheless thoughtfully designed to suit the plant-loving Batemans with a Roman peristyle, rhododendron (later fern) house, orangery and camellia house. Herbert Minton was a fellow orchid enthusiast whose nearby Minton Hollins tile factory supplied the house with ceramic flourishes. From the gracious Italian terraces the view across the lake was translated into the riotous colours of the Himalayan foothills by banks of newly introduced rhododendrons. Beyond this romantic introduction lay a voyage of discovery and excitement.

The Staffordshire blue-and-white willow-pattern wares of Josiah Spode and Joshua Heath captured the oriental appeal of Cathay, the old name for China, in the public imagination. At Biddulph the blue-and-white china story came to dazzling life. Cooke secreted 'China' within the 'Great Wall' which was extended by an outcrop of rocks covered in yews and pines; there is just one break in the wall. The path curves under a watch tower (p. 156, *below*, *left*), which was armed with two cannons, and passes through the first massive stone Chinese doorway. A golden bull with a disc dominates (p. 156, *above*, *left*), while dragons play at his feet: set in a curved exedra the bull is probably based on the bronze ox at the Summer Palace in Beijing. The whimsical dragons are outlined in the grass, their bodies filled with pink chippings and a beady jade eye. If you have ever longed to join the willow-pattern chase, Cooke magically converted it into reality: the oriental patterned bridge that crosses the Chinese waters offers a perfect vista towards the Chinese Temple and Tea Terrace. Then there was the rocky climb through a sea of Chinese tree peonies (that actually failed to thrive)

Above: The Cheshire Cottage
Opposite: The Chinese Bridge, Chinese Temple and Tea Terrace

Above, left: The Golden Bull
Above, right: The Egyptian Sphinx
Below, left: The Watch Tower
Below, right: The Ape of Thoth

to the Joss House, a shrine or temple to an idol – the origin of burning joss-sticks.

The second massive stone arch leads to steps down to the lake or past a giant frog set back in the wall to the Chinese Temple and then the Tea Terrace. It took Cooke and the Batemans two years to perfect – the delicacy of the carved woodwork, the decorative detailing of the grebes, dragons and bells set under and on the gorgeously upturned eaves, the dramatic roofline tiled with brilliant Minton Hollins tiles. Escape was possible at the end of the terrace via grottoes and subterranean passages that lead into the Rhododendron Ground or Pinetum. Waterhouse Hawkins sculpted the golden bull, stone frog, dragons and possibly the 'lions, kymans [sic] and other sundry Chinese monstrosities'. Academic argument continues over whether he meant a Chinese kylin or a Buddhist Lion of Fo – the former is a mythical beast with the head of a dragon with a single horn, hooves of a deer and a bushy tail; the latter come in pairs, the lion playing with a ball while the lioness has a cub. A lion was found during restoration. Hawkins later sculpted the beasts for the Great Exhibition, some of which survive in Sydenham.

A buttressed yew walk runs from the house above the Great Wall to a belvedere at the corner of the cherry orchard, Eastern Terrace, the stumpery and 'China'. The view is panoramic and yet cleverly 'China' is concealed as is the other exotic location, Egypt. Lying between these two nations at the base of the belvedere was the stumpery, formed from the upturned stumps of trees whose roots created eerie tentacles, the crevices filled with soil providing pockets for shade-loving plants such as ferns. Two pairs of sphinxes guard the entrance into 'Egypt' from the Eastern Terrace. These are not the Greek-speaking sphinxes of Bomarzo (pp. 22–7) and Schwetzingen (pp. 96–9) but lions with a pharaoh's head, copies of the original in Giza, which are also seen at De Notelaer (pp. 128–31) and Bataille (pp. 244–7). Silence reigns as you enter the 'Egyptian

Above: The entrance
to 'Egypt'

Court' between obelisks clipped out of yew and under the stone portal of the inner pyramid. Crouching in the inner sanctum is the massive Ape of Thoth (p. 156, *below, right*) who, as an associate of the Egyptian lunar god, is credited with inventing botany. Behind the Ape a passageway leads into a traditional half-timbered building – the Cheshire Cottage (p. 154) without a grinning cat. The smiling face here is the happy balance of horticultural erudition with exuberant architectural originality.

Dramatic over-the-top ideas cross-fertilise through nineteenth-century follies and rocky landscapes, such as the rock theatre in the grove created for the Margravine Wilhelmine at Sanspareil near Bayreuth, which in turn would be the inspiration for Charles Beistegui at Groussay (pp. 198–203).

Bateman's dazzling garden cost a fortune and the estate was saddled with a mortgage of £35,000 (about £1.6 million in today's money) when his son inherited it. Forced to sell in 1871, for more than a century the grounds deteriorated, until the National Trust took over in 1988 and restored them to their former glory.

MAITRE ADAM
LE
CALABRAIS
UN AN
A
FLORENCE
LES FRERES
CORSES
BERNARD
HISTOIRE
D'UN
CASSENOISETTE

Château de Monte-Cristo, Le Port-Marly

Madame Mélingue had been bidden to view the magnificent château her friend Alexandre Dumas had built for himself; she knew it was at Le Port-Marly west of Paris but did not know the precise address. She ordered the carriage driver to take her to 'Monsieur Dumas – Monte Cristo', and such was the fame of the book, *The Count of Monte Cristo*, that they trotted over without delay. Much amused by the incident, Dumas christened the architectural extravaganza that the architect Hippolyte Durand had built for him in 1846 the Château de Monte-Cristo. Dumas père (his son was to bear the same name) claimed to have spawned 400 to 500 literary works and, regardless of accuracy, he was indeed a prodigiously prolific and hugely successful author who, with Victor Hugo and Alfred de Vigny, formed a triumvirate of French Romantic literature.

The two sides of Dumas's character are expressed in the building of the lavish château and its accompanying modest Gothic retreat that he named the Château d'If. The house (*right*) was used for sumptuous entertainments that fulfilled his frivolous, spendthrift, generous, promiscuous and gourmand nature. The little building tucked away in its leafy retreat symbolised his professional dedication and efficiency; as Didier Decoin of the Académie Goncourt wrote: 'Alexandre Dumas mythographe devenu mythe' – 'Alexandre Dumas the legend writer became legendary.'

The diminutive Château d'If (*above and overleaf*) stands like a gingerbread house within sight of the exquisitely detailed main house that exudes the wealth that was enjoyed by the eponymous count and made by Dumas himself from the novel. Where the main house is decorated with busts of celebrated writers, this Forteresse de Poupée (Doll's Fortress) has some of the titles of his books and stories inscribed on its stonework (*opposite*) and has a statue of a dog in his kennel by the front door. It is surrounded by water – Dumas liked to watch the antics of his guests from the safety of his literal isle. The building is splendidly eclectic in its architectural styling: there are Gothic windows, a rose window, ornately carved bargeboards and Renaissance-inspired balconies. The interior arrangements were plain: downstairs a study where he could write and upstairs a little bedroom where he could rest, both simply furnished.

Dumas wanted a *parc anglais*, so using the natural undulating topography he created winding walks from which to experience a romantic atmosphere enhanced with grottoes, shell-work, cascades and water effects. A prodigious number of fish were introduced in the pools. In the words of Dumas: 'In the solitude of Monte-Cristo, I was in my own earthly paradise – I love the solitude of heaven on earth, that is to say a solitude accompanied by animals.'

Despite his acclaimed love of solitude and gentle fauna, this lavish party-animal finally reduced himself to bankruptcy and lost his terrestrial paradise.

Above: The Château d'If

Opposite: The titles of Dumas's works are inscribed in the stone insets

Overleaf: The Château d'If, also known as the Doll's Fortress

Quinta de Monserrate, Sintra

This palatial example of Anglo-Portuguese passion and extravagance, south-west of the historic town of Sintra, was the late eighteenth-century pleasure paradise of 'England's wealthiest son', William Beckford. He was the author of the semi-autobiographical novel *Vathek*, an 'oriental' story of a young caliph who initially dedicated his life to the quest for wisdom, power and beauty but then became drawn to wanton sensuality. Beckford used a small part of his huge fortune to landscape the wilderness of the mountains and make improvements to the *quinta* (the elegant and fruitful domain of a patrician), which was later described by Marianne Baillie in 1821 as: 'the most picturesque palace … [with] … every beauty and sublimity which Cintra has to boast'.

However, by 1856, the palace was no more than a romantic ruin when Francis Cook, an English textiles millionaire, first rented and then took possession of it seven years later. He engaged the services of architect James Knowles to build a new house in neo-Moorish style over the old footings.

The approaches are legendary: on foot past Beckford's Falls and the Ruined Chapel, through Fern Valley and along the Perfumed Path; or by carriage past the Cromlech and under the Indian Arch. One of the first sightings of the palace is the top finial on the dome which rises to 28m/91ft. The intricate architectural detail includes 1,176 treble arches ornately encompassing the building that are echoed by bands of leaf-and-tendril motifs. The palace receives its light through the ornate tracery of arched windows supported by carved columns.

As you enter the pillared portico there are eight columns with foliate spandrels bearing seven Moorish arches with fine lace and traceried detail. The eye is drawn up to twenty Gothic brackets grooved with machiolated treble arches that support the cornice. In elegant room after elegant room the effect is of light and grace.

The grounds were landscaped by William Stockdale, an artist and a Fellow of Kew, and William Nevill, a resident of Portugal. Acknowledged as a masterpiece of romantic Victorian naturalistic landscaping, the sweeping lawn from the house is reputedly the oldest in Portugal.

The Ruined Chapel in the Gardens has direct links to Gaspar Preto who named the estate after Our Lady of Montserrate near Barcelona and built the chapel on the site of a legendary Mozarabic tomb. Dom Luiz, King of Portugal, gave Francis the title of 'visconde de Monserrate' during the lifetimes of him and his son, and so he was known as Sir Francis Cook, a romantic honour for a devoted Anglo-Portuguese. Lord Byron, mad, bad and dangerous to know, was inspired by Monserrate for the Fairy Dwelling in *Childe Harold's Pilgrimage*.

Above: The Quinta de Monserrate at night
Opposite: A detail of the façade showing the traceried windows and minaret

Schloss Linderhof, Ettal

Set in the foothills of the Alps west of Ettal, Schloss Linderhof (built 1874–8 by Georg von Dollmann) is the smallest of (Mad) King Ludwig II of Bavaria's fairy-tale castles and the only one that was completed. It is an heroic folly, expressing its owner's abiding admiration for Louis XIV, and has a series of satellite – indeed stellar – follies that reflect Ludwig's love of poetry and opera.

The entrance is dominated by a large bronze statue of Ludwig's hero, and he even contemplated naming the castle Meicost Ettal, an anagram of Louis's saying 'L'État c'est moi' (I am the state). Although built as a private residence in an Alpine valley, it incorporated an ornate royal audience chamber and a hall of mirrors like that at Versailles. The exuberant creamy-white architecture can be described as neo-Baroque and neo-Rococo with a whipped topping of Atlas holding up the world (*right*), while the extensive gardens represent an *entente cordiale* of French, Italian, English and German designs.

The castle forms the axis of a cross-shaped design laid out by the Bavarian royal court gardener, Carl von Effner. The front overlooks a French-inspired sunken parterre and pool with a fountain which rises majestically to almost 30m/100ft. It is approached through ornate ironwork and down sweeping double steps. The centrepiece of the pool is a gilded sculpture of Flora gazing to the skies, her lap spilling over with gilded flowers and surrounded by frolicking putti. Although the scissor-shaped terraces that then ascend to the Temple of Venus (*opposite*) have smooth white walls, the effect is reminiscent of the Villa Garzoni in Italy. A sense of Italy is also expressed on either side of the terraces in the *giardini segreti*, green rooms enclosed by trellis work. On a straight axis with Flora and Venus there is a cascade of thirty marble water steps behind the castle leading to a gazebo (p. 166, *above*, *right*). Here the landscaping is formal but more naturalistic, with clipped hedges and mown grass that melt into the trees on the hillside. At the foot of the steps, a pool is dominated by a statue of Neptune, triton in hand, controlling galloping and rearing hippocamps, which is based on the original at Versailles.

Like Orsini at Bomarzo (pp. 22–7), Ludwig loved poetry and would read Ariosto, with his cousin Elizabeth, the Empress of Austria. Richard Wagner's compositions are cited as the inspiration for the high theatre of the dramatic designs of the Hundinghütte or Hunding's Hut, Grotto Theatre and Hermitage. The design for the Hundinghütte was based on the libretto from the *Ring of the Nibelungen*, the floor covered in bearskins where Ludwig would lie drinking mead with his retainers in a remake of the Valkyrie myths. The

Above: Schloss Linderhof
Opposite: Overview of the castle with the Temple of Venus

original burnt down, was rebuilt and then rebuilt again
in a different location; however, it is still recommended
to read and contemplate the images while listening to
the rousing strains of Wagner's 'Ride of the Valkyries'.

There is a waterfall and lake within the Grotto
Theatre formed from a 10m/33ft high cave that is
reached via a massive stone on iron hinges. Inside hang
spectacular stalactites that were artistically enhanced
when the king visited by being illuminated in many
colours. The grotto is said to be the first place in Bavaria
to use electricity, which was produced by one of the
original dynamos produced by Siemens-Schuchers. At
the back of the grotto is a huge canvas from Act I of
Tannhäuser, acting as a backdrop to the Königssitz or
shell-throne and there are tables and chairs made out of
coral. Like a fairy-tale prince, Ludwig took rides on the
lake in a conch-shaped boat. Good Friday was the
chosen day to visit the Hermitage so that he could sense
the consecrating effect of *Parsifal*.

At the Paris Exposition Universelle in 1867 Ludwig
had bought a Moorish Kiosk (*opposite, below*), designed
by the Berlin architect Karl von Diebitsch who worked
and studied in Egypt from 1862 to 1869. Ludwig had it

erected on the side of the Graswang Valley and added a
recess to hold a throne backed by three peacocks
crafted out of enamel and coloured glass. Like the
castle itself, it is painted white but with gilded dome
and minarets, topped by gilded crescents. The interior
was a fabulous version of the Alhambra's Court of the
Lions and markedly similar to Monserrate (pp. 162–3).
The Moroccan House (*opposite, above*) was also an
exhibition piece and was installed close to the Moorish
Kiosk in 1873. Ludwig used both buildings as places
where he could smoke a chibouk and transport himself
into the fictional world of the *Arabian Nights*.

Ludwig considered himself to be 'an eternal enigma
– that is what I want to be to myself and to others', but
the general consensus was that he was simply mad.
Building dream castles fed this folly. Location, location,
location are the three imperatives for a house and what
greater romantic legacy than this, nestling in pretty
woodland with views to snow-topped mountains and
(mostly) blue skies. There is perfection in the grand
transition from the realms of architectural art to the
realm of nature as art at Linderhof that eluded Ludwig
the man.

Le Palais Idéal, Hauterives

Between 1879 and 1912, in a back garden in Hauterives in the Ardèche region of rural France, a village postman painstakingly created a unique edifice of extraordinary individuality. Le Palais Idéal is concrete poetry on an epic scale infused with religious meaning and, after the death of 'Le Facteur Cheval', it became a shrine for the Surrealists.

A literate peasant, baker and postman who lived at a time when unremitting toil and rural poverty were the norm, Joseph-Ferdinand Cheval could be said to see the world in a grain of sand. In 1879 he noticed a beautiful stone on the Tersanne road after a rock fall; he wrapped it in his handkerchief and carried it home. Thereafter, each day, as he delivered post on his 32 km/20 mile round, he dreamt and gathered flat, long molasses (post-tectonic sediments) eroded by rivers, round pebbles, tufa and red porphyry. Over the next thirty-three years he used tons of stone, vats of shells and 3,500 sacks of cement to build what he initially christened 'Le Temple de la Nature', which, as Tim Knox has written in the Introduction, has a bizarre Angkor Wat-like appearance.

The exterior is an exuberant synthesis of many examples of grand architecture incorporating fantastic pillars and buttresses with ornate cornices that support finials, arches and crenellated towers. Poor but literate, Cheval travelled the world of art and design through the pages of illustrated magazines. He started with the east façade of his palace, which he called 'La source de la vie' (The source of life) with a fountain in front; it was constructed from cockle, snail and oyster shells with assorted stones cemented with white chalk. In a majestic hymn to nature, he added fantastic animals and exotic plants. He then added the Grotto of Saint Amédé in homage to the local patron saint. He furthered the theme of origins with 'La source de la sagesse' (The source of wisdom) for which he created an Egyptian tomb that he intended to be his and his wife's burial place. Sheltering in little niches he made pagodas and oriental temples suggesting a voyage towards initiation. He sculpted the rock wall into deer shut away behind first a stone door, and then ironwork, adding an inscription that the only source of wisdom was to be found in true contentment. His religious faith was affirmed in the Grotto of the Virgin Mary, where the Virgin Mary was surrounded by the four Evangelists. Then three giants of history whose size matches their greatness – Archimedes, the great Gaul Vercingétorix and Julius Caesar and at their feet two mummies, the goddess of liberty and the arch-druidess Vélléda. The Barbary Tower contains the reservoir and is surrounded by palms, olives and Barbary figs. Cheval then built a belvedere from which to admire his work and later the Villa Alicius where he and his wife lived after his retirement.

On the north façade Cheval exposed his creative soul by constructing Genesis, in many forms, with

Above: A grotesque detail
Opposite: The poem by Parassac that prompted Cheval to rechristen his Temple of Nature 'Le Palais Idéal'
Overleaf: The west façade

Above, left: The Pilgrimage

Above, right: Genesis

Below, left: Alpine Chalet, Hindu
Temple and Algerian Square House

Below, right: Le Facteur Cheval's
Testament

Opposite: La source de la sagesse

superb coloured shells. The world meets on the west wall (previous page) – a Hindu temple, Swiss chalet, Algerian square house, a medieval castle and a mosque. Five cultures are represented by their architecture, perceived by Cheval in inscriptions and symbolised by a stone bestiary. There are beasts such as bears, boa constrictors, crocodiles, lions and elephants. The interior of the Hindu Temple was a large grotto made up of smaller ones containing fossils he had discovered during his rounds as a postman. Over the entrance to the mosque he wrote 'The Spirits of the Orient are coming to fraternise with the Occident.' Emile Roux-Parassac, the Alpine Bard from Grenoble, wrote a poem to Cheval which he inscribed in 1904 – 'It is Art, it is a dream, it is energy … Your Palace of Superb Ideals.'

Cheval rechristened his Temple 'Le Palais Idéal' and its fame spread, postcards were produced and he employed a servant to help him give guided tours. He finally finished its construction in 1912 and in 1914 'Le Facteur Cheval' was granted permission to build a tomb for himself and his wife in a similar arrangement to Jack Fuller (*see* pp. 134–5). She died that year. He continued work until 1922 and died in 1924, the same year as the first Surrealist manifesto, in which André Breton defined Surrealism as a 'functional expression of thought … dictated by thought alone, uncontrolled by reason and outside any aesthetic or moral preoccupations'. In 1920 Breton had declared Cheval's work to be a precursor to Surrealist architecture; and painter and printmaker Jean Dubuffet considered it an early form of Art Brut (*see* La Maison Picassiette, pp. 194–7). In 1964 André Malraux, French Minister of Culture, classed this as the only example of Art Naïf and declared Cheval to be the first proletarian to enter into the history of modern art. In August 1937 Picasso visited and sketched twelve drawings entitled 'Le Facteur Cheval'. It had all started from one eye-catching stone and a disposition to dream.

Quinta da Regaleira, Sintra

'The nose of Europe whose face is Portugal' is a popular description for Sintra, a sprawling town northwest of Lisbon which, for royalty, Lisbon aristocracy and the wealthy aspiring middle class, is the resort of leisure and pleasure. The Quinta da Regaleira is Sintra's youngest but, in comparison with the other romantic

folly sites of Pena (pp. 150–3) and Monserrate (pp. 162–3), its most philosophical demesne. While the Palácio da Pena was the early architectural exemplar of the European romantic fusion of Arab and Indian styles, the later more philosophical Quinta da Regaleira encapsulates the history and characteristics of the Portuguese soul. Eighteenth century landscapers followed Alexander Pope's advice to 'consult' the *genius loci* or 'genius of the place'; in Portugal, and specifically Sintra, this equated to seeking the Lusitanian soul. 'Lusitanian', still used to describe Portuguese terrain and plants, originates with the noble actions of the ancient patriot Lusitano, who had refused to accept Roman domination but fought for the freedom of his native soil. The follies and setting of Regaleira celebrate these historic roots.

Above: The Tower

Opposite: The elevated walkway

In two purchases in 1893 and 1896, Dr António Augusto Carvalho Monteiro, nicknamed Monteiro dos Milhões (Moneybags Monteiro), bought the Regaleira Tower, Renaissance House, battlemented Greenhouse with 4ha/9 acres of gardens, coppice and orchards. He commissioned the Italian architect Luigi Manini who had worked at La Scala, Milan, to create a mansion of

philosophy that was sensitive and empathetic to the sacred and arcane roots of the landscape. The structure and decorative features of the palace, which was completed between 1905 and 1911, are an excellent example of the neo-Manueline style, a term used to describe the nineteenth-century Romantic Revival architecture of Portugal, equating with the British Arts and Crafts movement's devotion to medieval and Gothic traditions. Every surface at the Quinta da Regaleira is fabulously rich in plant motifs, spirals, twisted ropework and contrasting rough and masoned rocks (*opposite*).

Work on other buildings had started in 1898 when Manini hired stone craftsmen and sculptors from Coimbra, such as Mestre Gonçalves who had founded the Escola Livre das Artes e Desenho (Free School of Art and Design) and as sculptors the brothers José, Luís and Júlio da Fonseca from Sintra. The indigenous forest was romantically supplemented with plants and trees from all over the world, and from this Edenic scene an array of belvederes, galleries and balconies rose, while various grottoes and a well plunged into the depths of nature's soul. Throughout there are overt symbols that declaim Monteiro's conservative and monarchist allegiance as well as his Gnostic Christianity and Freemasonry.

Monteiro desired the visitor to go into the woods along the paths of humility, shadows, silence and rebirth, punctuated by operatic architectural aria devised by Manini. The first stage was pagan in the Egyptian House of Thoth, the god of wisdom, numbers,

music, astronomy, guardian of libraries and temples
who is closely associated with the Greek god Hermes
and Roman Mercury (*see* Biddulph Grange, pp. 154–7).
The house is decorated with a blue background mosaic
of several ibis drinking at a spring.

The Regaleira Tower (p. 175) hits a soaring note,
the effort of climbing the spiral staircase to its heights
rewarded by a breathtaking view of Paradise Regained.
Among the massive trunks and shady glades of chestnuts,
oaks and olives, the Celestial Terrace exudes a more
austere note. At the centre of the curving terrace an
ornately decorated arch opens to the grotto within;
climbing up offers a magnificent panorama. Monteiro
wanted to evoke a sensation of vision and intuition –
beauty lies in the eye of the beholder, so what memories,
what hopes are called to mind by stone, water, light,
shade, enclosure and open spaces?

All paths lead to the Menhir that equates with
Monserrate's Cromlech or standing stone, an upright
cult symbol of power and protection that dates back to
Portugal's megalithic culture. The mystery of where a

solid door might lead is a well-used dramatic device to
suggest a passage from the known to the unknown, from
the profane to the sacred, from safety into danger. A
stone door activated by a hidden mechanism provides
an entry into a womb-like underworld via a perilously
steep spiral stairway, galleried with columns, flights of
fifteen steps descending down nine levels. A Templar
Cross is inlaid in marble with an eight-pointed star – the
coat of arms of Monteiro at its base. A descent through
labyrinthine tunnels created in local rough-hewn granite
and sea-eroded stone has the added atmosphere of bat
colonies. The presence of bats can symbolise many
things: as cave dwellers they are symbols of immortality,
as nocturnal creatures they signify darkness and
melancholy, and, as mammals that fly like birds, they
represent a co-existence between opposites in alchemy.
The descent has close parallels with the levels in Hell,
Purgatory and Paradise in Dante's *Divine Comedy* (*see*
Bomarzo, pp. 22–7).

There are several symbolic references to the third
person or Holy Spirit in the Holy Trinity at Regaleira

(*see* Rushton Triangular Lodge, pp. 34–5). In the landscape there is a stone bench with a greyhound at each end, and five castellations on each side of the central figure of a woman who is probably Dante's Beatrice (*right*). This numerology can be read as the 5-1-5 of the *Divine Comedy* indicating *il veltro* (the greyhound) or *il Messo di Dio* (Messenger of God) announcing the coming of the Holy Spirit and the salvation of Man. The crypt of the Chapel is paved with tiles and has an underground altar resplendent with Templar Crosses and pentagrams whose five-pointed stars symbolise man with his arms spread out horizontally – the world in microcosm.

The discovery of Brazil during the reign of Manuel I brought vast wealth to Portugal and to Monteiro, so it is apt that Regaleira is richly neo-Manueline. The stunning Romanticism of the architecture and landscape are merely follies for the uninitiated, to date decoded by master masons but currently undergoing re-evaluation. Regaleira is operatic in the complexity of its Christian, Freemasonic and Portuguese mythic symbolism.

Quinta da Aveleda, Oporto

In the leafy hilltop town of Penafiel, along the Duoro Valley from Oporto, lies the Quinta da Aveleda, set in a landscape rich in sensual greens, with lush subtropical plants, venerable moss-covered buildings and the taste of refreshing *vinho verde*. Water is key to the design and philosophy of the gardens, exploited for its beauty in pools, streams and waterfalls. The follies here almost run the full gamut of nineteenth-century garden architecture.

While the oldest building on the site is the Chapel which dates back to 1671, the French-style house was built in the 1890s by Manuel Pedro Guedes, who surrounded the vast estate with a 3m/10ft high double dry-stone granite wall. The profiles of four Guedes sisters were carved by João da Silva on to one of the most celebrated fountains depicting the Four Seasons.

Adopting the principles of French formality, Guedes created avenues and walks, softened on either side by naturalistic English informality that was in harmony with the rugged Portuguese terrain. The main avenue is interspersed with cork oaks and, giving additional late-winter and spring colour, banks of azaleas, rhododendrons and camellias. It is traditional

Above: Interior of the Tea House
Opposite: An archway

for camellia petals to be scattered to create flowery carpets for Easter processions. In the centre of the main avenue is a seventeenth-century granite cross that originally stood in front of the parish church of Penafiel. It is set among palm trees, symbolically linking the everyday journey to and from the house with Christ's arrival into Jerusalem that is celebrated on Palm Sunday.

Of the two lakes by the house, the larger Forest Lake has two islands with extensive olive groves. One folly on the lake offers a view into Portuguese history. It is the window from which Dom João IV was officially proclaimed king in Oporto and had been saved when the Royal Palace was demolished in 1800; its carving of tendrils and masonry details are now outlined in moss and surrounded by trees. Architecture, water and religious symbolism combine in the fountain wall dedicated to Our Lady of Vandoma (p. 180, *above, left*) who is patron saint of Oporto. It was copied from one in the Benedictine monastery of Tibães.

A columnar fountainhead, heavy with symbolism, is topped with an overflowing basket of fruit and vegetation – the land's bounty. The four-sided plinth is supported by dolphins beneath which are four gnarled faces – green men. In the moist shade a confusion of massed plants have colonised – a symbol of fertility – whilst water flows from into four stone shells, also supported by dolphins in a quatrefoil shallow basin. The pale green colour provides a link with the other abundant liquid on this estate – the wine or *vinho verde* that was shipped from Aveleda to Brazil and Africa. Taking symbolism to extremes, it is also said that the

Above, left: A fountain wall dedicated to Our Lady of Vandoma
Above, right: The Goat Tower
Below, left: The Chapel
Below, right: Columnar fountain head
Opposite, top: Thatched cottage for geese
Opposite, below: King D. João IV's window

vicissitudes suffered by this estate such as good and poor harvests, political upheaval, lives and deaths in the family, were alleviated by the abundant presence of water which acted as a constant companion in meditation and in times of sorrow.

Romantic housing for animals is taken a step further than the duck castle at Pena (*see* p. 150–3). At Aveleda the geese have their own small thatched cottage (*opposite, above*), a rustic picturesque *cottage orné* set on an island in a lake, reminiscent of a Japanese tea house. The blossom of ornamental Japanese cherry trees enhances the oriental flavour. The goats are quartered in a rough stone circular tower (*above, right*) with a spiral outer walkway that gives access to their upper room. The rustic look is echoed in the surrounding iron fence wrought to look like tree branches.

The other thatched rustic building is for taking tea, its style reminiscent of what the French called 'Robinson' after the Irish garden writer William Robinson who promoted the use of local materials for garden structures. Could there be an inspirational thread? Robinson influenced the French and the French influenced the Portuguese. The interior of the Tea House (p. 178) is not as expected: apart from the hunting trophies in the form of antlers on the walls, there are numerous reptiles – giant lizards and snakes – colourfully produced in Portuguese pottery, writhing over the wood-lined ceilings. This is tea in the woods without the discomfort of a picnic – nearby a large mossy granite table and benches provide a setting with royal credentials, for it was here that the young Prince Luís Filipe took lunch with his tutor, Mouzinho de Albuquerque.

The prince and his tutor might have toyed with the etymology of *aveleda* which is said to stem from the abundance of the herb sage, *Salvia*, for today the follies are softened by moss which in oriental gardens stands for the wisdom of ages. So it might be said that the Aveleda follies are rich in sagacity.

MODERNISM & INDIVIDUALISM

Modern architecture became a recognised phenomenon by 1930 form should follow function and design should draw on a scientific and aesthetic appreciation of nature. The strictures of taste were exploded and, as the dust continued to swirl, Surrealist patterns emerged. Art and architecture encouraged the quest for original expression, ranging from the unschooled artist using whatever was to hand to highly trained technicians crafting the latest man-made materials.

The folly of daring to be different has richly rewarded I.M. Pei. As François Mitterand endorsed Pei's controversial Pyramid fronting the Louvre, he commented, 'At the base of all politics is the politics of culture.' Pei had pointed out to Jean Dubuffet, who coined the term Art Brut, the similarity between his sculptures and the ornamental rocks of classical Chinese gardens. Wacky ideas run like coloured threads through the weave of eclectic follies inspired by modernism and individualism.

Parc Güell, Barcelona

Pinnacled, turreted, modernist Moorish rooflines designed by Antoní Gaudí punctuate the skies of Barcelona and at Parc Güell are set against the steep, wooded slopes of the mountain foothills. Parallels can be drawn between the vibrancy of Italian Renaissance architecture fuelled by a new powerfully rich merchant

class and their early twentieth-century Spanish counterparts who were commissioning daring edifices, from mansions to shops, for the thriving commercial city of Barcelona.

The original design for Parc Güell was for sixty houses with private gardens set in a communal landscaped park of 17 ha/42 acres, linked by sinuous roads and walks. Despite altruistic intentions, only two houses were ever built. The park is enclosed by a curvaceous tile-topped wall, with the main entrance flanked by two pavilions that would not look out of place in a fairy-tale forest. On the right-hand side is the Porter's Lodge, which has an organic, squat look, built in local stone, with two medallions proclaiming Parc Güell (*left*), rising to a spiky tile-covered roof, a spire topped by a cross and a central turret with a red and white tiled toadstool. On the left of the entrance is the Office Building (*opposite*) with a blue and white toadstool echoing the colour of the sky

Above: An entrance medallion to Parc Güell
Opposite: The Office Building

and its scudding clouds, curiously offering symmetry by its very asymmetry. The application of *trencadís* (broken tiles) in kaleidoscopic patterns to walls, chimney pots and ventilator shafts here and throughout the park was mostly undertaken by Josep Maria Jujol. As a surface treatment it adapts beautifully to the local climate.

Eusebio Güell (pronounced 'Gway') was Gaudí's generous patron, and in 1900 the two men conceived the idea of a garden city in 'the neighbourhood of health' – Gracia – where the hills touch the city of Barcelona. In his individual 'Modernista' treatment of stone, tiles and intricate ironwork, Gaudí was heavily influenced by Spain's Moorish legacy and openly admitted to borrowing from neo-Gothic and Art Nouveau designs. Modernista in the sense of his admiration for natural forms and flowing lines, his vision was initially channelled into preparing coloured and exquisitely detailed architectural drawings; he would then work closely with the terrain. For, like Güell, he admired the English landscape and worked with the irregularities and dictates of the topography.

Moorish and Art Nouveau influences are most obvious in Gaudí's individualistic ironwork. Decorative iron gates and balustrading lead to a double staircase with a central water-spouting dragon, Python – defender of subterranean waters (p. 186) – but this somewhat benign, brightly coloured Python can be interpreted very differently from his namesake in the Apollo Fountain at La Granja (pp. 76–9), perhaps underlining the differences between commercial Catalonian Barcelona and royalist Castilian Madrid?

Behind Python, a snake's head against a red and yellow tiled background symbolises the Catalonian coat of arms and acts simultaneously as an overflow spout for water collected from above – utility and beauty in one.

From Python, the eye is drawn up to the massive Doric columns of the 'Hypostyle' that support the market place. Of the eighty-six columns, the capitals on the outer columns are carved with a motif that resembles a portcullis whilst the Doric pattern is adapted to a foliate or petal pattern on the inner columns (*above, left*). Jujol's work can be seen in the mosaic medallions that provide dramatic bosses between the columns, anticipating the work of the Dadaists. The area underneath offers shade and cool and is still often used for impromptu concerts. Gaudí designed the columns so that they cleverly disguise rain downpipes from the market place. The water is stored in a vast underground cistern and then recycled to 'green' the entire year round, hence Python's leafy trough, as well as irrigating other plantings.

The breadth of vision cannot begin to be appreciated as you climb up the inner stairs from the shady Hypostile, but taking one step on to the market place is like a revelation – spectacular views due east over Barcelona to the Mediterranean Sea. This vast central flat terrace was designed for communal dancing but no public kissing and cuddling! With its back into the rock, its outer side is edged with a curvaceous perimeter seat, brightly decorated with *trencadís*. Beyond

are waving palms whose trunks echo the natural rock, a motif that Gaudí replicated in stone for the subterranean galleries to the south of the market place.

Pathways take you to the house where Gaudí lived with his elderly father and orphaned niece and onwards under pergolas swathed notably in colourful bougainvillea and wisteria. Although only two houses were built, the walks to others survive, offering a climb up to the stark crest of the hill shaded by the greys and greens of pines, olives, eucalyptus, holm oak and privet. Lining the walk are 150 round stones that represent rosary beads so that you can enter into prayer as you ascend.

In 1988 Juan Bassegoda Nonell wrote succinctly: 'Gaudí understood that Nature used magnificent structural forms ...'

A Catalan to his innermost fibre, Gaudí would only communicate in his native tongue; born in the city of Reus in 1852, he died in Barcelona in 1926 while still working on his other great landmark, the Sagrada Familia.

Above, left: The ceiling of the Hypostyle Hall
Above, right: Covered walkway
Opposite: The dragon Python, the defender of subterranean waters
Below: Seating decorated with *trencadís* in the market place

Portmeirion, Gwynedd

Bill Bryson described the colourful village of Portmeirion near Penrhyndeudraeth in Gwynedd, Wales, as 'the most magical and ambitious folly built in the last hundred years'. For Bertram Clough Williams-Ellis, the architect who created it between 1925 and 1976, it was 'a home for fallen buildings' because, in addition to those he designed in an array of architectural styles as a pastiche of grand baroque, he also re-erected threatened historic buildings there. In reality it looks just like a film-set (*overleaf*), one famously associated with the '60s television series *The Prisoner*.

Williams-Ellis bought the site of Aber Iâ (Glacial Estuary) in 1925, a surprising and depressing name for a region that enjoys the benefits of the Gulf Stream Drift. He renamed it Portmeirion, 'Port' because it is on the coast and 'Meirion' because that is the Welsh name for its county – Merioneth. Photographs of scale models and plans were published in *The Architects' Journal* in 1926, and most of the buildings were complete by 1939.

Petrol pumps (p. 192, *left*) were few and far between in the 1920s, so in 1926 a National Benzole petrol pump was provided in Trinity Yard, tailored to Portmeirion tastes by having an early nineteenth-century painted pine amorphous figurehead with red cap and blue plume. The petrol theme was wittily continued by placing marble busts of the Duke and Duchess of Argyll, sculpted by Michael Rysbrack, on painted upturned petrol cans in alcoves overlooking the pool.

The Bell Tower or Campanile was built as an eye-catcher and public relations exercise that would draw attention to the great Portmeirion architectural adventure. It was designed by Williams-Ellis in 1928 to provide an introduction to the happy follies among which it nestles – that it succeeds can be seen in an overview of the town (*overleaf*). The tower rises elegantly from a medieval-style base in local stone topped with a two-storey Palladian section to house the bell; the chiming clock within had been rescued from a demolished London brewery. The rooftop complete with weather vane is classic in its simplicity.

When the Toll House was built on Battery Square in 1929, it marked the outer limit of the village and still has a bell that you can ring to attract the attention of the gate-keeper. A painted oak statue of St Peter (*opposite*) on the balcony shelters under a small metal canopy, which should have been bigger, but Williams-Ellis assured the foundry that manufactured it that St Peter would not mind. It has overhanging storeys and is faced in weather-boarding described by Williams-Ellis as 'that black weather boarded thing, looking rather Norwegian'. The woolpack sign is a sheep cut-out designed by his daughter Susan to advertise the Welsh Wool Shop within.

In 1941 Williams-Ellis purchased the adjoining

Above: The Gothic Pavilion

Opposite: St Peter on the balcony of the Toll House

Overleaf: An overview of Portmeirion with the Pantheon, the Bristol Colonnade and Campanile

Gwyllt Woodlands, noted for its excellent trees and exotic shrubs. He recommended building work in 1954 and continued until 1976, filling in architectural detail as well as constructing new classical and Palladian edifices – one of the Palladian tollbooths was his last building in 1976. Other dominant buildings are the Bristol Colonnade, added in 1959, and the Pantheon or Dome in 1961. The colonnade came from Arnos Court, Bristol, where it had been built for a Quaker copper smelter William Reeve in 1760, but had been badly damaged by bombs. Every stone in the dilapidated structure was numbered before it was transported and reassembled at Portmeirion. One of the two ogee cupolas that ornamented the ends was damaged, so Jonah Jones carved a replacement with a likeness of Williams-Ellis. The Pantheon made up for what was considered a 'dome deficiency' and in a delightful take on keeping the home fires burning, the portico is actually a Norman Shaw fireplace of red Runcorn sandstone from Dawpool, Cheshire, which Williams-Ellis had acquired in the late 1930s.

In 1963 Williams-Ellis decided to turn the centrally situated tennis court into an eclectic centrepiece to be called the Piazza; this included a gloriette, Gothic pavilion and Ionic columns supporting gilded Burmese figures which dance in the courtly style associated with Mandalay in the late nineteenth century, their liveliness heightened by their being so high above the ground. All are fine examples of recycling and providing a home for old buildings. The Gothic Pavilion (p. 189) was built out of a heavily damaged *porte cochère* (carriage portico) from Nerquis Hall in Flintshire; under the portico a pair of barley-twist teak columns support painted metal cut-outs which were to be viewed from the front only. The view across a formal pool is to the Gloriette, a Palladian portico and a fountain deriving from a colonnade salvaged from Hooton Hall in Cheshire. Its architectural inspiration came from Schönbrunn Palace near Vienna and it was designed to 'vivaciously contradict' the facing stable block. Its narrow profile is deceptive as it leads on to a balcony overlooking the village.

Williams-Ellis expressed his guiding principles as 'Cherish the Past, Adorn the Present, Construct for the Future' – which describes Portmeirion in its own individualistic way. His knighthood was celebrated in a cartoon called 'The New Arrival' by Hans Feibusch in which Sirs Christopher Wren, Nicholas Hawksmoor and John Vanbrugh greet him cautiously. On 28 May 1973, his ninetieth birthday was marked by Lord Harlech who unveiled a statue of a lion and voted Portmeirion a 'Good Thing'.

La Maison Picassiette, Chartres

The spires of Notre Dame de Chartres can be seen for miles across the flat plains south of Paris, an outward sign for pilgrims seeking this crucible for Christian worship. In the suburbs of Chartres lived a foundry worker and street sweeper, Raymond Isidore (1900–64), who was inspired by cathedral architecture and absorbed in religious symbolism. Magpie-like Isidore started collecting bright or interesting pieces of broken glass and ceramics, which he gradually piled up in his garden. In 1938 he started to adorn every wall, every surface, including furniture and household goods, in his newly built house with mosaics. The bedroom took the Isidores into the desert with a caravan of camels whereas the kitchen transported them to Mont St Michel. Isidore worked on the exterior walls (*overleaf*) and the outhouse in his garden until there was no surface left uncovered in this shrine to a beautiful mind.

Above: Self-portrait of Raymond Isidore with his wife, Adrienne
Opposite: The courtyard wall with some of the forty-four European cathedrals

Although entirely individualistic, spiritually and artistically, the effect is Gaudí (*see* Parc Güell, pp. 184–7) meets Le Facteur Cheval (*see* Le Palais Idéal, pp. 168–73). Jean Dubuffet attended the Académie Julian in Paris in 1918 but only dabbled in painting while working as a wine merchant until the Second World War. In the 1940s he coined the term Art Brut: he studied graffiti and the paintings of psychotics and pioneered the use of rubbish such as discarded newspapers, broken glass, and rough plaster daubed and scratched like an old wall. Presaging Pop Art and Dadaism, he defined this as art in the raw, the spontaneous outpourings of the ordinary man – consummately wrought by both Cheval and Isidore before the term existed. These two labouring men are linked in their exploration of the wonders of the world through the pages of magazines, books and postcards.

The dark hues of the Black Courtyard symbolise the Earth and Isidore's own humble work, the pebble-work underfoot replicating a mosaic. Not one but forty-four European cathedrals rise majestically on the main courtyard wall (*opposite*) that surrounds an image of the Virgin Mary – the mother of the Church whose birthday on 8 September Isidore shared. Immediately above her is an intricate depiction of the rose window and stained glass at Chartres's great Notre Dame Cathedral. Between 1953 and 1956 Isidore added a private chapel to the house. Washed with blue, which is symbolically associated with Mary and heaven, its mosaic depicts Jerusalem, Christ and floral symbols of Mary, such as roses and marigolds, juxtaposed with rural scenes of Chartres.

In the gardens and mosaic courtyards, there are images of people and portraits of Isidore and his wife, Adrienne, as well as over three hundred decorated flowerpots for annual planting to add more bright colours. The orchard has a replica of the Eiffel Tower under the shade of apple trees along with other towering monuments. The Garden of Paradise that he filled with sculptures was a later purchase. The garden has been described as a hymn to the themes of life, death and resurrection and to the importance of fidelity. In the house the ceilings are covered with motifs of giant

water lilies, roses and butterflies. There are frescoes of weeping willows, bouquets of flowers are offered from the walls and the individual petals on the cascading wisteria on the friezes are fashioned from porcelain. The bright red and yellow flowers and their leaves covering cupboard doors could have inspired the flower-patterned crockery of the 1960s or Laura Ashley dress fabrics of the '70s.

The name Maison Picassiette can be interpreted in two ways – Art Brut or Cubist perhaps: one is *pique-assiette* (plate-pincher) and the other is an amalgam of Picasso and *assiette*. What better association than Picasso whose passion was to swing the emphasis of taste towards dynamic power and vitality, rather than perfection, so that his paintings and ceramics evolved into the expressive use of blocks of colour. Picasso painted in Barcelona from the age of fourteen, in the shadow of Gaudí's architectural works and decorative *trencadís*, and he visited Le Palais Idéal. Whatever the genesis, the artist's name links naturally with *assiette* – not just a plate but surely a gloriously colourful piece of faience.

Above: The kitchen

Left: A mural in the passage

Opposite: The front of La Maison Picassiette

Château de Groussay, Montfort l'Amaury

On the Rue de Versailles about 44 km/27 miles south-west of Paris lies the Château de Groussay whose follies and interiors are the masterly legacy of cosmopolitan Charles de Beistegui. Money no object is one of the foundation blocks of a folly and the wealthy Beistegui devoted his life to perfecting every facet – architectural, furnishings, fabrics and *fabriques* – for his personal pleasure. His consummate good taste and attention to detail gave rise to contemporary awe, expressed as the '*goût* Beistegui' (the Beistegui taste), rivalling and perhaps surpassing the '*goût* Rothschild'.

The style Beistegui pioneered in the 1940s (for he continued to decorate lavishly throughout the Second World War, oblivious to its devastations) became one to which the post-war rich aspired. In November 1944 Cecil Beaton described the building as having 'no great architectural pretension'; it was effectively a blank canvas with huge potential and no restrictions. Rectangular, pedimented and shuttered, it had been built in about 1815 by the Duchesse de Charost, and later Russian owners had painted the stucco pink and the shutters green. The transformation was undertaken with the help of the Cuban-born fashion designer turned architect, Emilio Terry, who incidentally had supported an unknown, struggling Salvador Dalí. Terry was a neoclassicist who ignored the Vitruvian requirement of *firmitas* (firmness) in preference for 'commodity' and 'delight' (*see* Romanticism and Innovation, p. 133).

Born in Paris to Mexican parents and educated at Eton, Beistegui was the presiding genius who liked to work comfortably ensconced in bed: his inspirations were first put into watercolours by the Russian Alexandre Serebriakoff that were then prepared as maquettes and constructed by Emilio Terry.

The Palladian Bridge was built in 1955, and its positioning was decided by hauling around a full-size painting until the perfect location west of the château was found. Not Palladian as at Stowe (pp. 64–9) but more Robert Adam as in the Tea Bridge at Audley End in Essex. A pyramid, based on that of Caius Sestius in Rome, with a double flight of steps to a terrace over an Aphrodite-inspired shell grotto was sited beyond it, where it is serenely reflected in the lake (*following pages*).

The small island on the lake in front of the château was used as the location for a three-tiered Pagoda inspired by eighteenth-century French *chinois* models such as that at Santeny in the Val-de-Marne by Terry in 1963. It is octagonal, built in wood with a copper roof; however, in order to match the Île de France skies, the roof was painted slate grey. To the east a long avenue of horse chestnuts leads to a column topped with an observatory dome that echoes the one in the Place Vendôme in Paris.

In his comprehensive library Beistegui possessed plans executed by the French neoclassical architect

Above: The Observatory Column

Opposite: The three-tiered Pagoda

Overleaf: The Pyramid and Shell Grotto, which were added in 1968

Louis Jean Desprez dating back to 1797, which had been commissioned for the Swedish King Gustave III in 1781 and simplified for the Swedish royal palace of Drottningholm into copper tents built as guardhouses. Beistegui liked the more detailed and flamboyant doorways and trim in the original designs which he copied for the Tartar Tent. The interior, known as the Salle Hollandaise (*left*), is made of copper and lined throughout with over 10,000 blue-and-white Delft tiles showing flowers, birds, stylised birdcages and an intertwining ivy leaf motif.

The high theatre of the detail extended to staging dramas inside and out. The Théâtre de Verdure (Green Theatre) is approached through a stepped hedged alley into a labyrinth with a central round temple. A clipped hedge draws you through a topiary doorway, fashioned with a prominent clipped keystone and a pair of urns; then stone-edged steps lead into the auditorium of the living theatre (*opposite, above*). Beistegui had the idea of making a *théâtre de verdure* at Groussay from visiting the gardens and Teatro di Verdura created by Oliviero and Lelio Orsetti, in 1652, at Villa Reale, Marlia, near Lucca. Within the green alcoves of the theatre he incorporated figures from the Commedia dell'Arte: Punchinella, Columbine and Pantaloon. In opulent contrast the theatre inside the château, inaugurated in 1957 with a production by the Comédie Française (*opposite, below*), which is based on the Margravine's theatre at Bayreuth and the Youssoupov theatre at the palace of Saint Petersburg, has been described as 'dreamy baroque'. Here Terry fused the works of Andrea Palladio and Claude Ledoux in a way that was much admired by the Surrealists. The blue background hosting three tiered balconies, flounced puce draperies, Murano glass chandeliers and ornate gilding showcased the glittering audience and their host as much as the players. There is a sense of his Cuban childhood and Irish parentage fuelling this passionate realisation of his patron's reveries. Truly a *folie de grandeur*.

Above: The interior of
the Tartar Tent
Opposite, top: The Green
Theatre
Opposite, below: The interior
of the theatre in the house

Parco di Pinocchio, Collodi

Above: The 'Good Fairy' in disguise

Opposite: Four black rabbits carrying a coffin

The historic town of Collodi lies on the Lucca to Florence road, straddling the historic borders between the Grand Duchy of Tuscany and the Republic of Lucca. The town is famed for the dramatic, Mannerist-meets-Baroque garden structure that frames the Villa Garzoni. Legend recounts that the young Carlo Lorenzini learnt to read and write in the kitchens of this villa where his grandfather was manager. Did its latent allegory and fantasy influence him when he wrote *Avventure di Pinocchio* in 1883 under the pen name of Carlo Collodi? Seventy years later it was decided to create a park in Collodi that re-enacted Pinocchio's adventures and his world where morals and fantasy combined to encompass the reality of Italian street life and the beauty and isolation of the Tuscan countryside. The landscape architects Renato Baldi and Lionello De Luigi were joined by Pietro Porcinai, who was born in Florence and grew up in another fabulous Italian garden – the Villa Gamberaia at Settignano.

The journey at the Parco di Pinocchio starts with Emilio Greco's magical 5m/16ft tall bronze of the graceful 'Good Fairy' gently supporting the awkward Pinocchio, the spiral airiness of the sculpture topped by her falcon that saves the hapless hero. The tell-tale nose is prominent and, as in the story, grows and diminishes as the pilgrimage unfolds. Through a pageant of pebble and coloured broken-tile mosaics, designed by Venturino Venturi, the wooden puppet, having deserted his honest father Geppetto, always chooses the easy path which, as every classical and religiously trained mind knows, leads to vice and ruin. In the first *piazzetta di mosaici* (mosaic courtyard), a part of the wall is edged in white stone like a puppet theatre, depicting our naive hero with the 'Showman' and 'Pulcinella', the latter of whom could equally peel off and join the journey to Apremont (*see* pp. 218–21).

The scoundrel 'Fox and Cat' that haunt Pinocchio are a threatening presence in mosaic and sculpture, depicted lying, cheating and murdering. Pinocchio is left to slowly hang by the neck, but the 'blue-haired child' that is in fact the 'Good Fairy' in disguise (*left*) commands the falcon to cut the knot around the puppet's neck and has him carried to her *casina*. What happens to children who will not take their bitter medicine? The fairy calls in four rabbits carrying a coffin (*opposite*) to graphically show the future for boys who will not heed sound and virtuous advice. The good and bad characters that animate the story and the cricket that represents Pinocchio's conscience have been sculpted by Pietro Consagro. In this undoubtedly modernist park, his final piece, an excessively long-nosed Pinocchio, acts as a traditional reminder to the mendacious.

La Scarzuola, Montegabbione

A road winds through verdant Umbrian countryside from Montegabbione, passing beneath the high township of Monte Giove, across the valley and up to

La Scarzuola. Here St Francis of Assisi founded a convent in 1218, where recent restorations have unveiled a fresco of the saint in levitation. Francis created a shelter from the local reeds – *scarza* – and so the site was named Santa Maria della Scarzuola; he planted a biblical bush of bay and Marian roses, and a spring, an emissarium, a veritable font of life, gushed forth. Conventual centuries passed until this sacred landscape was acquired by a Milanese architect who between 1958 and 1978 designed a complex in the wooded hills (*above*) of theatre spaces in what he called the Ideal City conception. Here the architecture of an eccentric mind included a glittering Crystal Pyramid, topped by a shining star (p. 213), a latter-day, Masonic, reflection on the clarity and symbolism of the original saintly spring.

Above: Tomaso Buzzi's Città Ideale in the woods at La Scarzuola

Opposite: The Theatres of Water and Bees

Tomaso Buzzi (1900–81) was truly a twentieth-century man. Others described him as frenetic, with a restless breadth of interests, cultural ambition and intellectual fickleness, whilst he called himself a 'prince of architects'. He viewed architecture as frozen music, and the restless breadth of his interests included refrains from Europe's folly builders and their references. Like the creators of the Château de la Bastie d'Urfé (pp. 18–21) and Bomarzo (pp. 22–7), his intellectual journey was inspired by the allegorical landscapes in the Humanist tract *Hypnerotomachia Poliphili*. His neo-Mannerist exuberance was stirred by the Villa d'Este (pp. 28–33) with its echoes of Hadrian's Villa, especially the Rometta Fountain. There is a sense of both when choosing the route to take at La Scarzuola's three openings into trellised avenues, where the central one is to 'Love' which leads to the island-boat-temple about to set sail for the shores of Cythera.

Buzzi's love of the eighteenth-century *capriccio*, a device that fools the eye into believing that buildings have been raised one on top of the other, is evident (*overleaf*) in his architectural compositions that echo the conceits painted by Giambattista Piranesi, designed by the architect Claude Nicolas Ledoux and modestly created at Hestercombe in England. Then, while socially and intellectually a world apart, the works of Buzzi and Le Facteur Cheval (pp. 168–73) share an indefatigable Constructivist dream, a three-dimensional outlet for inscribed quotations and moral maxims. Buzzi was also a compulsive collector of frescoes, canvases, busts, theatrical scenery, lapidary and ephemera that are used to unusual and almost Surrealist effect.

Unlike Portmeirion (pp. 188–93) or Hundertwasser at Rogner Bad Blumau Spa (pp. 230–5), Buzzi's Città Ideale or Città Buzziana was not designed as a physical shelter or to accommodate happy communes, although it does have a small population. A respected modernist architect and interior designer, his Roman contemporaries derided his eccentric frenzied folly. The idealistic dream in his 'autobiography in stone' was to allow the mind and body to wander freely and

Above, left: The Gate of
Heaven
Above, right: Palladian
window in the Theatre of
the Bees
Opposite: Detail of buildings
in the Città Buzziana
Overleaf: The Colosseum,
Borromini-style lantern,
the Pantheon and
the Crystal Pyramid

ethereally through the architectural contrasts of the
sacred (convent) and the profane (theatres) that are
conceptualised in a surreal stack of buildings. Buzzi
converted the convent into a home for himself. He
confided in his diary how his 'creature', his 'stony ruin'
progressed; how it represented a 'message in a bottle
entrusted to the waves of time' and 'idea-stones which
speak of me'. The stark reality was that he failed to
supervise the local contractors who did not use the
specified materials or put in foundations or drainage.
By 1978 the reality was far from ideal as much was
collapsing into ruins. The design plans and records
survived, entrusted to Buzzi's protégé and disciple,
Marco Solari, who continues to bring Buzzi's vision to
fruition, but on firmer foundations.

The seven theatres in the Città Buzziana parallel
Shakespeare's seven Ages of Man, laden with, and for
the cognoscenti illuminated by, symbols and codes,
references and quotations. The drama of this cityscape
is revealed and concealed, the eye can voyage freely
whilst the body has to follow where the routes lead.
From the contemplative green it is essential to keep
looking around to read the architectural metaphors –
the Gate of Jonah, a circle of walls, the Tower of Time,
the unfinished Temple of Eros, footings of the House-
Capital, the Temple of Apollo, the towering Column of
Meditation and the Temples of Flora and Pomona. The
Gate of Jonah is a wide-jawed beast that symbolically
marks the transition from one world to another, very
much in the spirit of Bomarzo (pp. 22–7). The story of

Jonah and the Whale is one of the best-known biblical
tales, replicated in Pinocchio's adventures where he
finally finds and rescues Geppetto, suggested in the real
whalebone arch at Stancombe Park (pp. 142–3) and
here carved out of tufa to look like worn bone.

For his empire Buzzi chose a world of classical
architecture that could be viewed from a hanging
garden balcony. The scene is dominated by the Acropolis
on an eminence under which are modern-day
catacombs which Buzzi compared to a termite's nest
that, rather than hiding Christians, shelters classical
buildings – the Parthenon, Pantheon, Colosseum,
Temple of Vesta, Arch of Titus and Tower of the Winds.
Finally, the eye is summoned back up to the Bell Tower.

The Theatre of the World extends into the landscape
while the vast all-seeing 'third eye' – the window of the
soul and Masonic symbol – watches all, standing out in
relief centrally placed on the podium below the stage.
The sound of frozen music includes a sweet hum in the
Theatre of the Bees – *buzzicare* is the Italian for the busy
buzz of bees, a play on his name in both English and
Italian. This small theatre was modelled on La Scala in
Milan, and there is a similarity with Manini's work at the
Quinta da Regaleira (pp. 174–7).

The broad welcoming exedra of the Theatre of
Water has striking parallels with the Maritime Theatre
at Hadrian's Villa. The waters are used to amplify the
actors' voices and to offer a mirror to the architecture.
This is followed by the unroofed Temple of Apollo, at
whose core there is the skeleton of a cypress, also known

Above, left: Clock in the
Tower of Time
Above, right: Star patterns and Buzzi
family coat-of-arms in the Theatre
of the Bees
Below, left: Door of the Coat-of-
Arms House with queen bee
Below, right: The Tower of Babel
Opposite: Architecture among
the clouds

as the funeral tree because it never regenerates after being felled. As this cypress has been struck by lightning it is alone in having had direct contact with the skies.

Another emblem of man's folly across the centuries, also used at the Désert de Retz (pp. 120–3) and the Château de Groussay (pp. 198–203), is the Tower of Babel (*below, right*). Here it hangs from four wings with the Staircase of Knowledge spiralling through its core, the parapet fashioned into small bookshelves. The associated confusion of pride and multilingual babble is ordered into the Crystal Pyramid (*opposite*) containing the seven octaves of the musical scale.

Dialectica is one of the primary liberal arts which Buzzi uses to architectural effect: his designs balance a melancholic-connected discourse between death and eternity, the finite and infinite. Is this a city or a garden? It is a modern landscape where, rather than performing a purely decorative function, nature plays an organic, constructive and deconstructive role. Brian Pentland has laid out the gardens in harmony with the original convent and parkland of the Città Ideale. You cannot hear the discussion or the music but they are inferred by the order of the demonstrably cultured classical designs counterbalanced by the use of 'ruinous' materials – tufa and iron – and the uncompleted chaos. In architecture the ruin is the form closest to a return to nature, in which, in its decline, nature and culture come perilously close to each other.

Buzzi (and his disciples) have bridged the centuries of architectural follies with exuberant Mannerist mouldings and monsters, linking the Renaissance intellectual maze with Surrealist labyrinthine itineraries. He called it his 'folly, great or small', a place 'to which I have anchored my present and my future, … [the] posthumous architecturally grandiose tomb of my passions, intellectual and otherwise, and of my dreams …'. The spires of the sheltering belt of cypress trees provide an evergreen backdrop and a timeless representation of immortality.

The John Fairnington Cement Menagerie, Branxton

The hope and humour of the Cement Menagerie are in stark contrast to the palpable melancholy of the field of the Battle of Flodden just half a mile away. This multi-coloured menagerie of more than three hundred full-sized animals, as well as birds and human beings, was devised by retired joiner John Fairnington for the delight of his disabled son, Edwin. A folly created out of paternal love has come to represent a fine example of Art Brut.

It was during a Scottish holiday that Fairnington admired the sculpture that adorned great gardens – hence his copy of William Brodie's Ram Fountain at Moffat in Dumfriesshire. Feeling inspired to try a little light do-it-yourself, Fairnington started work at Branxton in 1961. While a little further north, Ian Hamilton Finlay from 1966 was perfecting the classical allusions of his concrete poetry at Little Sparta, here the carved words are a pick and mix of sentiment, quotations and dedications. The animals are larger than the Scottish bard's 'wee timorous beastie' but Robert Burns's poetry is celebrated in a shrine dedicated to him.

Despite his cerebral palsy it was decided Edwin should stay at home; his mobility in the Fountain House was helped by a tricycle while, outside, his imagination was fed by his father's artistic endeavours. The story goes that John Fairnington started with models of the doves in his aviary and, if so, there is a splendid resonance with the dove arriving with an olive branch in its beak to herald the release of the animals in Noah's Ark. Each animal began life as a full-size drawing which was interpreted with the help of a former colleague,

James Beveridge. The larger animals such as zebras, giraffes, hippos and elephants were created from the ground upwards, supported by iron stays for their legs; all the creatures were fashioned in galvanised wire-netting and filled with paper and other refuse. Cement was applied in layers like *papier mâché* and then (brightly) painted. So super-size animals roam with rabbits, dogs, stags, sheep and pandas around the ankles of such eminent personages as Sir Winston Churchill, cigar in hand. Lawrence of Arabia on his camel shares this enclosure with local champion shepherd and sheep-dog trialler, Bob Fraser. Many follies explore and contrast the sacred and the profane, and here religious figures sit alongside Disney characters in an ecumenical fiesta.

The cement menagerie grew and progressed until Edwin's death in 1971; then as the final poignant memorial to this young man's short life John Fairnington created the 'Memory Corner' before he died in 1981. This Northumbrian gem shares the passionate exuberance and unstoppable creativity of Le Palais Idéal (pp. 168–73) and La Maison Picassiette (pp. 194–7) and, like them, it is folly with a smiling face.

Above: Rhinoceroses – parent and child

Opposite: Some of the three hundred animals in the menagerie

The menagerie

Château d'Apremont, Apremont-sur-Allier

Located some 16km/10 miles from Nevers in the Berry region is the Château d'Apremont, which the French refer to as a garden of the Thousand and One Nights. Its roots lie deep in Anglo-Burgundian history, close to the Allier, one of the rivers that flow along the Loire Valley. Against this rich green canvas elegantly exotic follies grace the river as it winds through the spacious park, among them the Turkish Pavilion which evokes the banks of the Bosphorus in the age of the Ottoman Empire and the Pagoda Bridge, which transports visitors to the lakes and islands of China.

In 1970 Gilles de Brissac inherited the ten-acre estate of Apremont from his grandfather Eugène Schneider, an ironworks owner, who had restored the park in the 1930s. Brissac was a garden lover and professional garden designer, for whom the wealthy and cultured Charles de Noailles had been a seminal influence. Over the years, Gilles and Elvire de Brissac created a setting with lakes, a cascade and lawns with clumps of trees, shrubs and flowers as the backdrop for the restoration of surviving buildings and the execution of new follies.

The landscape undoubtedly pays homage to the classic *jardin anglais* and Vita Sackville-West's twentieth-century garden at Sissinghurst, although the greens of the soft plantings and grey stones of the cascade on the site of the former stone quarry are enlivened by the 'Genie of the Waters', a modern brightly coloured Cubist figure sculpted in wood by the Portuguese artist Baptista Antunes.

Catherine and Alexandre Serebriakoff were both authorities on the influence of Japanese art on nineteenth-century art and design. Alexandre Serebriakoff, a decorative artist and architect, was the man who realised and recorded many of the twentieth century's decorative dreams. His work at Apremont and at Groussay (pp. 198–203) has the elegance of the classical folly yet sports modern colours. In contrast to Monet's ubiquitous Japanese Bridge, in 1985 Serebriakoff designed a vermilion, yellow and eau-de-nil Chinese Bridge, topped by a delicate two-storey pagoda rising to a gilded pinnacle (*opposite*). The bridge spans the water, standing in stark but bright contrast to the dreamy blue of the lake and soft mounds of the shrubs and trees on each bank. The brilliance of vermilion on Chinese garden structures is also used to good effect at the Château de Canon (*see* p. 2).

The Turkish Pavilion (*above*) is simple in concept but detailed in its decoration: painted externally in blue and white stripes, the four doors are of finely wrought iron rising to an ogee, and the friezes have gilded and jewelled quatrefoils. It is doubly ornate as the structure seems to float on the second lake in which it is mirrored. Inside the Moorish and Turkish themes were beautifully

Above: The Turkish Pavilion

Opposite: The Pagoda Bridge

Above, left: The Chinese lake and Pagoda Bridge

Above, right: The Belvedere

Opposite: One of the eight tiled panels in the Belvedere

executed by Serebriakoff: mirrored panels set in ornate Moorish arches reflect the ironwork of the doors, alternating with paintings of Turkish women, such as a dancer and a sultana shaded by an outsized parasol. The skirting panels are painted like *mihrabs* (prayer niches) and contain Turkish-style flower still lifes or faux marble.

By contrast, the last folly to be built was the Russian-inspired Belvedere (*opposite*), which is in the neoclassical style with white painted columns and tangerine stucco topped by a cupola with a gilded pineapple. White stone-edged wide grass steps lead up to the point where all can be surveyed across the landscape: the peaceful image of grazing white Charente cattle and down to the fairy-tale rooftops of the medieval village and the River Allier. The Belvedere closes the triangle between the castle, the highest point in the park and the Turkish Pavilion. Inside, the walls are painted in a light lime-green decorated with branches of arbutus and pots of roses; above are eight panels of tile-work that are reminiscent of the *azulejos* of the Palácio da Fronteira (pp. 54–7) in

their humour and narrative. They were painted by Alexandre Serebriakoff and made by a local atelier – Art Montagnon. They chart the journey of four characters from the Commedia dell'Arte dressed as Pulcinella: the first scene is the embarkation at Venice and the eighth their rapturous arrival at Apremont. They voyage to Mandarin China and a Saharan oasis in Africa, pass under the flight path of a condor at Machu Picchu, dwell in the shadow of an oriental onion-domed palace complete with Bengal tiger in a cage, toy with a giant crab in the South Seas, and gaze at gazelles in the shadow of Mount Kilimanjaro.

In the last panel (*opposite*), with swans swimming in and out of the tableau, white suited top-hatted masked figures, with a curious look of the French Foreign Legion, gesticulate enthusiastically towards the Chinese Bridge, the Turkish Pavilion and the château. Gilles de Brissac spent part of his childhood in England and retains affectionate memories of swans, hence the tile motif and real black swans on the lake around the Turkish Pavilion. Like swans on a lake, the follies lend serenity to the landscape.

Sheep's Barn, near Malmesbury

While cycling through the peaceful lanes of Wiltshire, Colin Stokes sustained horrendous injuries from a drunken driver and made legal history when he received compensation. In July 1989 he converted this into a 2ha/5 acre field near his cottage in a tiny hamlet in Wiltshire and invested in some sheep, headed by a ram of primitive Celtic breed. However, the fleece of the Castlemilk Morrit, as it is called, is very short so Stokes orchestrated some careful crossing until a new fleecier breed emerged, which he named 'Braydon' for the sacred spring and ancient well that are the source of the local Braydon Brook.

To reach his sheep field Stokes had to cross a 20ha/48 acre all-weather gallop, where the owner wanted the central area to be cleared of surface stones so the horses could graze. As he went back and forth to his field, Stokes collected twenty or thirty barrows of stone a day, with which he constructed an artistic range of cairns. Gradually, from his hands a palatial shelter grew organically on substantial concrete footings: above the ground-floor lambing shed he created a bedroom so as to be close at hand and then lofts for storing hay and fleeces. There is a small pan-tiled building for concerts (*opposite*), and dovecotes with cooing doves protected from rats by the protruding stone courses, where even a little owl took up residence. A favourite architectural conceit is the flying buttress (*overleaf*), which is in tune with the organic growth of the building. Stokes feels it is akin to epiphytic roots on plants.

The windows allowed Stokes to display his skills as a stained-glass artist: the Four Seasons are represented by wild flowers, while a greenfinch decorates the semi-circular eyebrow window. The Four Elements are symbolised by a badger sett for Earth; barn owls for Air; the sunset for Fire and flooded fields for Water.

During lambing Stokes lived with the flock, helping the ewes through their labours, and for nine years he spun, dyed and wove their wool. Beneath the sheep grazing in the neighbouring field lay Forest Marble, a thin shale-like Cotswold stone that is a valuable roofing material. Considerably more profitable than sheep, the stone was quarried and, with the further threat of a landfill site, Stokes's idyll ended. He and the sheep moved north but, tragically, seven years later, after sixteen years perfecting 'Braydon' sheep, they were all culled during the foot and mouth outbreak – the frightening folly of fear.

Another move and the phoenix is rising once again in Moffat in Dumfriesshire in the form of an organic concert hall.

Above: The lambing shed
Opposite page: The Hermitage and the Dovecotes
Overleaf: The Sheep's Barn

A Dacha, near Ludlow

The prose of Tolstoy and Dostoyevsky inspired the building of this antique emblem of Russian romanticism, a dacha with glistening domes amidst a private Shropshire arboretum. Its initial use in 1990 was more prosaic: to store Robin Parish's collection of Morris and Ferguson tractors and general machinery associated with the arboretum.

Images of dachas abound but the reality of designing and building one was masterminded by two men: Steve Wilson who had built wooden houses in Oregon and since progressed to barn conversions and film sets; and Roger Thomas who had spent a year studying in Russia and was working with the film producer Michael Howells on set design. The 'stage' here is a flat site between a bank and above Hollow Meadow, with romantic views over the lake and on to the distant hill fort of Oaker.

Parish noted that Orthodox churches have five symbolic domes – four for apostles and a central one for Christ – an idea he copied. Wilson and Thomas used materials to create the domes that are magnificent examples of twentieth-century ingenuity and recycling,

Above: A dome made from a recycled water tank
Opposite: The shingles made out of local green oak
Overleaf: Three of the five domes

Art Brut at its zenith. The central dome is gilded fibreglass, a further two are former hot water cylinders rubbed down and varnished (*above*), one is made from ply and a blue one with stars is directly interpreted from Orthodox examples (*overleaf*). The shingles on the roofs are hand-cleft green oak which gives an (intentionally) uneven effect (*opposite*).

Dostoyevsky was a *dachnik* or dacha owner, also known as 'summerfolk' because the word derives from the Russian to give and dachas were usually offered as a gift to city dwellers from landowners. In 1842 P. Furman, writing on Russian architectural sources, referred to the dacha as an 'imprint of poetry'. With the aid of books on Russian wooden buildings, this Salopian dacha evolved with authentic exterior and interior additions, providing two bedrooms off the central octagon and a top-floor octagonal bedroom beneath a lantern-lit dome, as well as a Bath House with stove and dry sauna.

There are self-sown birch trees around but none of the angst of *The Cherry Orchard*; a magnificent cedar of Lebanon fell in 1989, its wood used to line the interior. The exterior is clad in local softwoods. The hearth is a Russian-style stone-surrounded stove and the walls have paintings by the Russian artist Kyrill Sokolov, whose wife translated the poems of Alexander Blok.

A thatched eighteenth-century hermitage complete with hermit stood about 400 metres or yards west of the dacha until 1930. In the sense of tranquillity and an individual imprint of poetry, Robin Parish's folly has succeeded it.

Rogner Bad Blumau Spa, Bad Blumau

Of this 'folliferous' spa village in south-eastern Austria, its architect Friedensreich Hundertwasser expounded: 'In former times painters painted houses. Today painters have to invent houses and the architects have to build after the paintings because there are no more beautiful houses.' Friedensreich Stowasser was born in Vienna in 1928. At the age of twenty, he made his first speech ('Everybody must be creative') and a year later embarked on the first of many extensive travels. He developed his own style in tune with nature, often addressing his audiences in the nude, and adopted the name of Hundertwasser.

Hundertwasser has been described as the Painter-King with five skins: the Epidermis – literally his bare flesh; Clothes – how we individually portray ourselves; Houses – under a living roof that was at one with nature; Identity, which included family and home country – he married several times unsuccessfully and travelled the world studying nations; and finally Earth – ecology and nature. For an English audience how fortunate that he identified five not four! Hundertwasser drew up a list of six global sites that displayed 'exemplary, healthful, contemporary architecture', two of which are Gaudí's buildings in Barcelona (*see* Parc Güell, pp. 184–7) and Le Palais Idéal (pp. 168–73).

Sinuous, curvaceous concrete buildings are great in frost-free environments such as Barcelona, but harsh winters call for reinterpretation. When Hundertwasser was commissioned by Robert Rogner to design the Hot Springs Village for Blumau, the original conception was a two-storey development incorporating an allotment-garden type, in which the wide variety of dwelling units would create lots of nooks and crannies. Hundertwasser fought to prevent the landscape being overdeveloped by a tide of terraced and individual homes, and seized the chance to realise his vision to build energy-saving homes in harmony with nature. He had expressed his dreamy vision for towns of the future in one of his earlier paintings, *Rolling Hills*, a Surrealist fantasy that took root in a modern landscape. He made a model for Blumau, in which he further developed these 1970s concepts. By 1991 he was working on the architectural project, and construction started in 1993, with a grand official opening on 10 May 1997.

The buildings' exteriors are smoothly rendered, the switchback walls that surround them capped and the exposed stone immaculately pointed. The bright blocks of colour are reminiscent of Baltic and Russian maritime towns and villages (*opposite and above*) – curious in a land-locked country. The undulating colour-washed walls under living roofs are entirely functional, cool in summer, warm in winter, and ecologically sound. A walk on the wild side takes on a new meaning when the productive hilly roofs create new space for nature and offer meadow and forest links from one part of the town to the next (*overleaf*).

It was his biggest project to date and colourfully incorporates his philosophy expressed in newly conceived architectural forms such as the self-explanatory eye-slit house (*opposite*, *below*), the forest-courtyard house, the

Above: A cone tower

Opposite: Apartments with a 'living' roof

The 'shifted-hill houses'
style

Above: Balconies providing tiny
private spaces
Opposite, top: The 'rolling-hill' style
Opposite, below: 'Eye-slit
houses' style

snail house, the rolling-hill (*opposite, above*) and shifted-hill houses. His longing for romanticism and creativity was fulfilled as he watched the residents and their visitors breathe 'forest and meadow air not concrete air'. If the eye is the window of the soul, the eye-slit houses look 'healthful' and welcoming, seamlessly blending into their landscape.

Zeal is one of the defining features of a twentieth-century folly builder, and the zealot Hundertwasser classed ugliness in architecture as a dangerous environmental toxin. He recognised that creativity results when the modern longing of people for a home and a life in harmony with nature was fulfilled; the outcome when natural rhythms and individual human creation were united was a good house. There is a symbolic and practical intention in building beneath the earth; damage caused by churning up the precious countryside is repaired naturally as the roofs take root. Far from creating a new generation of cavemen, with modern technology every comfort is available and the light values are excellent. Hundertwasser claimed that maintenance was simplified by being able to walk up on to the roof to carry out routine tasks.

Through personal presentations, models, plans and the written word Hundertwasser religiously espoused his crusade. Vienna turned him down as they anticipated that his designs would attract too many tourists wishing to view the human experiment. He encapsulated the built environment being at one with nature when he composed these two refrains and responses:

The residents are proud of their good conscience regarding nature. Everything horizontal under the open sky belongs to nature.

Here this has become reality. Man must give back to nature what he unlawfully took away from her down below in building the house and put it on the roof.

Here this has become reality.

Swarovski Kristallwelten, Innsbruck

In the heart of the rocky Austrian Tyrolean Alps a cornucopia of multifaceted crystals is wrought by the company originally created by Daniel Swarovski in Wattens near Innsbruck. Naturally, diamonds are a girl's best friend, but crystals are amiable jewels of light, reflective and reflecting, whether from a chandelier, a paperweight or an ornamental eye. A showman was needed to mark the centenary of the Swarovski company in 1995. With a background in the theatre, pop music industry and installation art, André Heller undertook the fantastical design of the celebratory Kristallwelten (Crystal Worlds).

From a green landscape, transformed in winter by the white of snow and ice, crystal-clear water cascades from a behemoth's mouth. Two glinting crystal eyes, under heavy eyebrows, oversee the approaching hordes of visitors entering its cavernous belly. Ruminants may have two stomachs, but this creature has six chambers on three levels that cover 0.2ha/½ acre, digesting and showcasing a mind-boggling array of crystal thinking.

A crystal witch casts spells in front of white calligraphy on black, the Leviathan spews lighted crystals like jellyfish tentacles and words appear on a rhythmically pulsating imaginative script of crystal spirals (*right*) created by Paul Seide, an American glass virtuoso. Cutting-edge artistic facets are displayed in works by famous figures such as Salvador Dalí, Andy Warhol and Niki de St Phalle.

At the heart of André Heller's Green Man is a world record beating crystal, weighing in at 62kg/137lb, a staggering size of 310,000 carats, 40cm/15½in. in diameter with a hundred light-catching facets. The labyrinthine nature of the exhibition is cut by a central crystal wall that rises a sparkling 11m/36ft high by 42m/138ft long, its cavity filled with 12 tons of glittering crystal stones. The twinkling Milky Way inspires the 'Planet of Crystals' and observations from the 'Crystal Dome'. The 'Crystal Meditation Room' was designed by the musician Brian Eno so that light and sound can transport visitors into another state of being. The drama is heightened by the colourful Venetian underworld where crystal-studded mannequins strut on the platforms of the 'Crystal Theatre' devised by Susanne Schmogner. Rather than using a crystal ball, palm reading can be undertaken on a grand scale outside in the park where Heller has formed a maze in the shape of a giant hand whose life, love and health lines are etched in evergreen trees.

Fabrizio Plessi has created a video installation 'Dream the dream – whose dream is it anyway?' Swarovski Kristallwelten is an upbeat confident reverie – hard-edged, bright, fantastic and foolish and a magnet for those in need of retail therapy.

Above: A calligraphic crystal sculpture
Opposite: André Heller's Green Man

Westonbury Water Gardens, Pembridge

The tranquil beauty and babbling of the Westonbury old mill stream at Pembridge in Herefordshire attracted a man with bottle in the late 1960s. Richard

Above: The Stone Tower
Opposite: Inside the Fernery
Overleaf: The Fernery

Pim like many a folly builder has found that his ideas take longer to materialise than planned, and he is still adding to the multicoloured dome (*opposite and overleaf*). The eye is not deceived: this sphere is created out of empty glass bottles from a variety of sources, cemented to create a kaleidoscope of muted colours for the ferns that are gradually being introduced within. Following publicity about his folly-fuelled exploits, an elderly man telephoned Pim to offer eighty-five blue bottles, the outcome of the glass of sherry consumed each Sunday by his wife as she cooked lunch. Friends have christened the folly the 'blotto-grotto', and continue to toast it with empty bottles.

Pim is a hydrogeologist with a fine-tuned under-current of knowledge which has permeated the scheme. Whilst the old leat or man-made channel continued to feed the mill pond, twenty-five years of overseas work meant this site remained a holiday home adorned with brambles and nettles. Happily, this irregular tenure provided the opportunity for Pim to develop an innate understanding of the landscape. Finally, in the late 1990s, personal circumstances forced him to channel his energies into this ancient site on to which he has grafted modern folly and fantasy in tune with the scenery, his first building being the African Summerhouse in 1997.

Rescuing the nineteenth-century waterwheel from the corn mill inspired serious architectural folly thinking. Between 2000 and 2002 he built the Stone Tower (*left*) so that he could recycle the waterwheel to drive a belt with little buckets into a trough which empties into two tanks. These tanks feed the two cheerful gargoyles and grim man's head that spout from the top of the tower. A mason dressed the stone, but Pim built the battlements and the actual carving was undertaken by him. The grim man was designed as a self-portrait but his hefty eyebrows and outsize eyes have been likened to those of Leonid Brezhnev. Doves with architectural taste are attracted by four elegant doors complete with door steps, their fluttering and cooing adding to the atmosphere.

The god of wine, Bacchus, sadly so often only associated with the folly of alcoholic excess, would make an ideal godfather for the 'blotto-grotto': he is also a divine figurehead for the civilising effects of wine as a means to companionable pleasures and conversation. So a toast to the modern individual!

The Pavilion, Oare House, near Marlborough

Wiltshire is famed for the glorious eighteenth-century follies of Stourhead, wonders wrought in stone, pebbles and shells – what sublime and awful sentiments might have been evoked 250 years ago at the sight of this cutting-edge folly built in glass and concrete. In 2005 The Pavilion received the Georgian Group Architectural Award for 'New Building in a Georgian context'. Praising its innovative design, when viewed from the eighteenth-century house, the citation noted that it serves as 'an eye-catcher ... bravely contemporary in its design but also entirely harmonious in its setting'.

The Pavilion's patrons are Henry and Tessa Keswick, who describe themselves as 'Scots in the English landscape by virtue of China', and the architect is the Chinese-American I.M. Pei. One of the late twentieth century's most successful architects, Pei has dared to be different, such as with his classic late modernist skyscraper for the John Hancock Mutual Life Insurance Company in Boston; whilst his controversial Pyramid fronting the Louvre in Paris, inspired French President François Mitterand to comment: 'At the base of all politics is the politics of culture.' The Keswicks had voyaged into the Japanese mountains to Pei's masterly Miho Museum to experience his sensitive combination of architecture and nature in a mutually supportive way.

Early in his career Pei had worked with the property developer William Zeckendorf, whose company specialised in producing site models so that clients would fully understand their designs and the impact that they would have on their surroundings. He greeted

the Keswicks with a model in a box – a heated glass pavilion of clean, clear lines, brimming with every twenty-first-century comfort.

Lying some 400m/1300ft from the house, The Pavilion has the angular look of a pagoda but its scale and interiors are that of a modernist princely tree house. Here the landscape grazes harmoniously around the cruciform concrete trunk and the electric glass doors allow a seamless entry from mown grass, and then a gracious ascent up a grand staircase into the spreading glass canopy. Octagonal, with four open-plan rooms that each has a glass sliding door, floored in oak under a complex glass roof, any greenhouse effects are neutralised by a delicate wood-grained aluminium grillage.

Queen Victoria's consort and promoter of innovative engineering, Prince Albert, would have marvelled at this latter-day Crystal Palace for modern individuals.

Above: I.M. Pei's contemporary eye-catcher seen against the Marlborough Downs
Opposite: Glass and steel wrought by the latest technology

Château du Champ de Bataille, Le Neubourg

Champ du Bataille is far from being a battlefield. The landscape has axes of power which stretch out from the château echoing France's 'heroic age' under Louis XIV and the dynamism of Versailles. These heroic roots provided the inspiration for the upbeat modern replanting by interior designer turned luxurious hotelier Jacques Garcia. Jean de La Varende encapsulated both the philosophy and outcome of Garcia's creation when he wrote: 'Here vastness reigns. The scenery only intervenes after power has been declared.' The result is a homage to the Baroque settings seasoned with an intellectual snobbery that might test the Académie Française.

Above: The Pantheon
Opposite: Le degré minéral
Overleaf: The Round Pond

Power visibly and philosophically progresses in designed landscapes through seven *degrés* (stages), from Mineral, Vegetable, Animal, Humanity, Conscience and Light to the intangible Spirit. Stone is used to evoke the first *degré minéral* around the chateau courtyard and the Grande Terrasse leading to a classical portico on the right, to the left an *allée* of sphinxes, the traditional symbols of an arcane territory. Then onwards down steps where two formal pools called the 'Cabinets de Marbre' (Marble Cabinets) flank the path. You are now on a journey designed to intrigue and play with your mind and the real folly in this landscape is not to be able to understand its iconography. The *degré végétal*, for example, stretches along an axis leading to a circular basin (*overleaf*) that represents the original ocean, not forgetting the circle is symbolic of the divine. The

Groves of Eden and Erebus, which decoratively frame Les Dentelles, lozenges of lace-patterned box-hedged beds that symbolise germination, line the route to the 'Ocean'. In Eden it is straightforward to read the well-ordered trees as the perfect paradise before the Fall of Man, and this side is terminated by a greenhouse with two squares – one dedicated to Apollo (sun and day) and another to Diana (moon and night). Erebus is a more complicated story. As the son of Chaos and the brother of Night, he is darkness personified, his name used for the gloomy underground cavern through which the shades of the dead had to walk en route to Hades. The Grove of Erebus is the antithesis of Eden, with chaotic, wild, self-seeding arboreal effects.

Passing the Ocean on the left, the journey takes you into the animal stage where the Swan Pool evokes the importance of birds, ornamented with a Temple of the Riches of Leda. Her riches came when Jupiter, disguised as a swan, ravished and impregnated her with two eggs. These hatched into two sets of mythological twins: Castor and Clymnestra and Pollux and Helen. Humanity lies opposite in the Pantheon mirrored in its square pool, the square symbolic of the hand of man.

Man's vocation, represented by parallel channels of water – temporal and spiritual lives – cuts through the landscape past the Green Theatre. Grand water steps (*opposite*) take the human conscience from terrestrial concerns to a celestial existence. The reflection of light from the mirror surface of the canal symbolises the radiance of the spirit which culminates in the sphere that crowns a column at the furthest point.

El Teatro, Villa Padierna, Marbella

Marbella near Málaga is a seaside town for the smart set, and the Villa Padierna is a luxury hotel designed by Ed Gilbert as a palace for modern grandees. Classical buildings and Moorish gardens evoke Andalusia's history, and in 2004 Gilbert started to construct an architectural extravaganza in front of the hotel, a crowd puller of Roman dimensions. This was championed by an enlightened entrepreneur who became his patron, Don Ricardo Arranz de Miguel and his wife Dona Alicia, daughter of the Marquis of Villapadierna.

The climate is perfect for open-air concerts and performances and in what better setting than an amphitheatre seating five hundred people. Gilbert harbours a fear of 'dark' theatres so, even if there are no live shows, the space is designed to be a constant spectacle in its own right – animated by day and lit at night (left and opposite). Pulling the plug on a performance has a whole new meaning here where the orchestra pit doubles as a fountain basin. The sculpting of water was inspired by the wondrous effects at the Villa d'Este (pp. 28–33) and the Cascade House at Chatsworth in Derbyshire. Gilbert likes to play with the elements: Water in canals, pit and jets; Earth contrasted in patterned stone, local rough travertine Olivillo and smooth marble Macael; Fire in the reflection of the noonday sun; and Air – the breeze gently rustling the enclosing cypresses and titillating the fountains. The architect paid detailed attention to synchronising the water and light effects so that the arching, fizzing, bubbling jets in the orchestra pit pool are colourfully choreographed.

Further jets create an arched crystal crossing to the central cascade at the back of the stage that draw the eye to a small basilica. Mirrored glass and cross bars on the basilica door are arranged so that at night the lighting creates a spiritual experience as the audience sees the form of a crucifix, which is echoed in the golden cross on the roof. The eight monoliths in Blanco Macael marble standing 3.5m/12ft high were quarried locally in Almeria; they form the multi-purpose backdrop which is reminiscent of Stonehenge. Apart from their stark architectural magnificence they act as acoustic sound boards and can be used for scenic projections.

Owing to the god's Olympian greatness, in ancient times statues of Jupiter were used only in public places, and here, with a lance and an eagle at his feet, he holds a commanding position (*opposite and overleaf*). Lined up with the basilica door, the classical god faces the Christian God Almighty.

In Praise of Folly was written by Erasmus in 1509; he noted that by '…definition wisdom means nothing else but being ruled by reason; and folly, by contrast, is being swayed by the dictates of the passions'. He also deliciously described pleasure as the 'seasoning of Folly'. Sculpture and fabric design swayed Gilbert towards architecture: with his patron, Arranz, and the master builder, Rafael Sepulveda, they have channelled their passions into geometric reasoning to create an architectural extravaganza.

Above: Seating in the Amphitheatre
Opposite: Jupiter presiding over the Amphitheatre
Overleaf: From the Theatre towards the Chapel

AUSTRIA

Rogner Bad Blumau Hotel & Spa
A-8283 Bad Blumau 100
Tel. + 43 (0)338 3 5100-0
www.blumau.com
By kind permission of Rogner Bad Blumau Hotel & Spa

Schloss Hellbrunn
Fürstenweg 37, A-5020 Salzburg
Tel. + 43 (0)662 82 03 72 - 0
www.hellbrunn.at
By kind permission of Schloss Hellbrunn

Swarovski Kristallwelten
Kristallweltenstrasse 1, A-6112 Wattens
Tel. + 43 (0)522 451080
www.swarovski.com/kristallwelten
By kind permission of the owner

BELGIUM

De Notelaer
Notelaarsdreef 2, 2880 Hingene
Tel. + 32 (0)3 889 69 20
www.notelaer.be
By kind permission of the owner

FRANCE

Château d'Apremont
Parc Floral d'Apremont
18150 Apremont-sur-Allier
Tel. + 33 (0)2 48 77 55 06
By kind permission of the owner

Château du Champ de Bataille
27110 Le Neubourg
Tel. + 33 (0)2 32 34 84 34
By kind permission of the owner

Château de Monte-Cristo
1 avenue John Fitzgerald Kennedy
78560 Le Port-Marly
Tel. + 33 (0)1 39 16 49 49 (information)
www.chateau-monte-cristo.com
By kind permission of the owner

Château de la Bastie d'Urfé
42130 Saint-Etienne-le-Molard
Tel/fax: + 33 (0)4 77 97 54 68
By kind permission of the Conseil Général de la Loire

Château de Canon
14270 Mézidon-Canon
Tel. + 33 (0)2 31 20 05 07
By kind permission of the owner

Château de Groussay
Rue de Versailles
78490 Montfort l'Amaury
Tel. + 33 (0)1 34 86 94 79
By kind permission of the owner

Désert de Retz
30 rue de Gramont, 78240 Chambourcy
Tel/fax: + 33 (0)1 30 74 47 51
By kind permission of the owner

La Maison Picassiette
22 rue du repos, 28000 Chartres
Tel. + 33 (0)2 37 34 10 78
By kind permission of the Musée des beaux-arts de Chartres

Le Palais Idéal du Facteur Cheval
26390 Hauterives
Tel. + 33 (0)4 75 68 81 19
By kind permission of the owner

Parc de Jeurre
91150 Morigny-Champigny
Tel. + 33 (0)1 64 94 57 43
By kind permission of the owner

Pagode de Chanteloup
Route de Bléré, Boîte Postale 317
37403 Amboise Cedex
Tel. + 33 (0)2 47 57 20 97
By kind permission of the owner

GERMANY

Herrenhäuser Gärten
Herrenhäuser Strasse 4, 30419 Hanover
Tel. + 49 (0)511 168-47743
www.hannover.de/herrenhausen
By kind permission of Herrenhäuser Gärten

Schloss Sanssouci
Maulbeerallee, 14469 Potsdam
Tel. + 49 (0)331/96 94 202
www.spsg.de
By kind permission of Stiftung Preussische Schlösser und Gärten Berlin-Brandenburg

Schloss Linderhof
Linderhof 12 , 82488 Ettal
Tel. + 49 (0)88 22-92 03-0
www.schloesser.bayern.de
By kind permission of Bayerische Verwaltung der staatlichen Schösser, Gärten und Seen

Schloss Schwetzingen
Schloss, Mittelbau
68723 Schwetzingen
Tel. + 49 (0)62 21 53 84 31
www.schwetzingen.de
By kind permission of Schlossverwaltung, Schwetzingen

Wörlitz Park
Förstergasse 26, 06786 Wörlitz
Tel. +49 3 49 05-2 02 16
By kind permission of the owner

IRELAND

Belvedere House
Mullingar, Co. Westmeath
Tel. + 353 (0)44 9349060
By kind permission of the owner

The Wonder Barn
Castletown, Celbridge, Co. Kildare
Tel. + 353 1 628 8252
By kind permission of the Department of Public Works

Larchill Arcadian Gardens
Dunshaughlin Road, Kilcock, Co. Kildare
Tel. + 353 1 628 7354
www.larchill.ie
By kind permission of the owner

ITALY

La Scarzuola
05010 Montegabbione, Terni, Umbria
Tel/fax: + 39 (0)763 837463
By kind permission of Marco Solari

Parco di Pinocchio
Via San Gennaro 3, 51017 Collodi (PT)
Tel. + 39 (0)572 429342
www.pinocchio.it
By kind permission of Fondazione Nazionale Carlo Collodi/Grandi Giardini Italiani

Reggia di Caserta
Viale degli Atlantici 12–14, Caserta
Tel. + 39 (0)824 316610
www.reggiadicaserta.altervista.org
By kind permission of the Ministero per i Beni e le Attività Culturali

Sacro Bosco
Bomarzo, 01020 Viterbo
Tel. + 39 (0)761 924029
www.bomarzo.net
By kind permission of the owner

Villa Barbarigo Pizzoni Ardemani
Via Barbarigo 15
35030 Valsanzibio di Galzignano, Terme
Tel. + 39 (0)498 059224
www.valsanzibiogiardino.it
By kind permission of Grandi Giardini Italiani

Villa d'Este
Piazza Trento 1, 00019 Tivoli, Rome
Tel. + 39 (0)774 312070
www.villadestetivoli.info
By kind permission of the Ministero per i Beni e le Attività Culturali/Grandi Giardini Italiani

Villa Nazionale Pisani
Via Doge Pisani 7, 30039 Stra (VE)
Tel. + 39 (0)49 502270
www.grandigiardini.it
By kind permission of the Ministero per i Beni e le Attività Culturali/Grandi Giardini Italiani

Villa Palagonia
Piazza Garibaldi 3
90011 Bagheria, Palermo
Tel. + 39 (0)91 932088
By kind permission of the owner

Villa Torrigiani
Via del Gomberaio 3
Camigliano-Capannori 50012 (LU)

Tel/fax. + 39 (0)583 928041
By kind permission of the owner

THE NETHERLANDS

Kasteel Rosendael
Rosendael 1, 6891 DA Rozendaal
Tel. + 31 (0)26 3644645
www.mooigelderland.nl
By kind permission of the owner

PORTUGAL

Palácio da Fronteira
Largo de São Domingos de Benfica 1
1500-554 Lisbon
Tel. + 351 21 778 20 23
*By kind permission of Fundaçao das Casas de Fronteira
e Alorna*

Palácio da Pena
Estrada da Pena, 2710-609 Sintra
Tel. + 351 21 910 53 40
By kind permission of IPPAR/Palácio Nacional da Pena

Quinta da Aveleda
Apartoda 77, 4564-909 Penafiel
Tel. + 351 25 571 82 00
www.aveleda.pt
By kind permission of the owner

Quinta de Monserrate
Estrada de Monserrate, 2710-405 Sintra
Tel. + 351 21 923 73 00
www.parquesdesintra.pt
By kind permission of the owner

Quinta da Regaleira
Rua Barbosa du Bocage, 2710-567 Sintra
Tel. + 351 21 910 66 50/9
By kind permission of Fundaçao Cultursintra

SPAIN

El Teatro, Hotel Villa Padierna
Ctra. de Cadiz, Km. 166, 29679 Marbella
Tel. + 34 952-889-150
www.ritzcarlton.com
By kind permission of the owner

Jardines de Aranjuez
Plaza de Parejas, 28300 Aranjuez, Madrid
Tel. + 34 91 891 1344
www.patrimonionacional.es
By kind permission of Patrimonio Nacional

La Granja de San Ildefonso
Plaza de España 17, San Ildelfonso, Segovia
Tel. + 34 92 147 0019/ or 92 147 0020
www.patrimonionacional.es
By kind permission of Patrimonio Nacional

Parc Güell, Montana Pelada, Barcelona
By kind permission of Barcelona City Council

UNITED KINGDOM

Barwick Park, Barwick, Somerset
Tel. + 44 (0)1935 462462
By kind permission of South Somerset District Council

Biddulph Grange
Grange Road, Biddulph
Staffordshire ST8 7SD
Tel. + 44 (0)1782 517999
www.nationaltrust.org.uk
By kind permission of the National Trust

Bramham Park, Wetherby
West Yorkshire LS23 6ND
Tel. + 44 (0)1937 846000
www.bramhampark.co.uk
By kind permission of the owners

Brightling Park, Brightling, East Sussex
(Brightling–Burwash road, at latitude
50 57 44 and in longitude 0 22 42E)
By kind permission of the owner. Private residence.

A Dacha, near Ludlow, Shropshire
By kind permission of the owner. Private residence.

The John Fairnington Cement
Menagerie, Branxton, Northumberland
By kind permission of the owner. Private residence.

Goldney Hall
Lower Clifton Hill, Bristol BS8 1BH
Tel. + 44 (0)117 903 4880
By kind permission of the owners

The Pavilion, Oare House
Nr Marlborough, Wiltshire
By kind permission of the owner. Private residence.

The Pineapple, Dunmore House
Dunmore, Stirlingshire, Scotland
By kind permission of The Landmark Trust

Mussenden Temple
North Derry Office, Hezlett Farm
107 Sea Road, Castlerock
Co. Londonderry BT51 4TW
Tel. + 44 (0)28 7084 8728
www.nationaltrust.org.uk
By kind permission of the National Trust

Portmeirion
Portmeirion Gardens, Portmeirion
Gwynedd LL48 6ET, Wales
Tel. + 44 (0)1766 770000
By kind permission of Portmerion Ltd.

The Royal Pavilion
4/5 Pavilion Buildings
Brighton BN1 1EE
Tel. + 44 (0)1273 292812
By kind permission of the Royal Pavilion

Rushton Triangular Lodge
Rushton, Kettering
Northamptonshire NN14 1RP
Tel. + 44 (0)1536 710761
www.cnglish-heritage.org.uk/visits
By kind permission of English Heritage

Sheep's Barn, nr Malmesbury, Wiltshire
By kind permission of the owner. Private residence.

Stancombe Park
Stancombe, Dursley
Gloucestershire GL11 6AU
Tel. +44 (0)1453 542815
By kind permission of the owner. Private residence.

Stourhead
Stourhead Estate, Stourton
Warminster, Wiltshire BA12 6QD
Tel. + 44 (0)1747 842020
www.nationaltrust.org.uk
By kind permission of the National Trust

Stowe Landscape Gardens
Buckingham
Buckinghamshire MK18 5DQ
Tel. + 44 (0)1280 823334
www.nationaltrust.org.uk
By kind permission of the National Trust

Wentworth Woodhouse
Wentworth, Rotherham
South Yorkshire S62 7TD
Tel. + 44 (0)1226 742041
*By kind permission of the Fitzwilliam (Wentworth)
Estates*

Worcester Lodge
Badminton South
Gloucestershire GL9 1DD
By kind permission of the owner. Private residence.

Westonbury Water Gardens
Westonbury Mill, Pembridge
Herefordshire HR6 9HZ
Tel/fax. + 44 (0) 1544 388650
www.westonburymillwatergardens.com
By kind permission of the owner

All information correct at the time of going to press

INDEX

BIBLIOGRAPHY
——————————————————

Ayres, Patrick, ed., 'Wentworth Woodhouse: A Landscape of Georgian Monuments', *New Arcadian Journal* 59/60, 2006

Bazin, Germain, *Paradeisos: The Art of the Garden*, Cassell 1990

Caine, Margaret and Gorton, Alan, *Cotswold Follies and Fancies: A Guide to the Curious, Whimsical and Romantic*, S.B. Publications 1998

Bredekamp, Horst, *Vicino Orsini und der heilige Wald von Bomarzo: ein Fürst als Künstler und Anarchist*, Werner'sche Verlagsgesellschaft, Worms 1985

Chastel, André, *Culture et demeures en France au XVIe siècle*, Conférences essais et leçons du Collège de France, Julliard 1989

Coffin, David R., *The Villa d'Este at Tivoli*, Princeton University Press 1960

Le Conseil Général de la Loire, *Claude d'Urfé et La Bâtie: L'univers d'un gentil-homme de la Renaissance* 1990

Headley, Gwyn and Meulenkamp, Wim, *Follies, Grottoes and Garden Buildings*, Aurum Press 2003

—*Follies: A National Trust Guide*, Jonathan Cape 1986

Holmes, Caroline, ed., *Icons of Garden Design*, Prestel 2001

Howley, James, *The Follies and Garden Buildings of Ireland*, Yale University Press 1993

Kingsbury, Ida, *Castles, Caliphs and Christians: A Landscape with Figures*, Associação Amigos de Monserrate 1994

Listri, Massimo and Cunaccia, Cesare M., *Giardini e parchi italiani*, Fabbri 1995

Macaulay, Rose, *Pleasure of Ruins*, Weidenfeld and Nicolson 1953

Neves, José Cassiano, *The Palace and Gardens of Fronteira*, Quetzal Editores M.T./Scala Books 1995

Pozzana, Mariachiara, *Gardens of Florence and Tuscany*, Giunti 2006

Sande de Freitas, João and Constâncio, Raul, *Trees of Monserrate*, Associação Amigos de Monserrate 1997

Restany, Pierre, *Hundertwasser: The Painter-King with the Five Skins*, Taschen 1998

Saudan, Michel and Saudan-Skira, Sylvia, *From Folly to Follies: Discovering the World of Gardens*, Abbeville Press 1988

Sitwell, Sacheverell, ed., *Great Palaces*, Weidenfeld & Nicolson 1964

Snoek, Jan A.M. et al., *Symbolism in 18th Century Gardens: The Influence of Intellectual and Esoteric Currents, such as Freemasonry*, OVN 2006

Spencer Jones, Rae, ed., *1001 Gardens you must see before you die*, Quintessence 2007

Sotheby's, Vente Château de Groussay, PF9001, 1999

Taschen, Angelika and Hundertwasser, Friedensreich, *Hundertwasser Architecture: For a more human architecture in harmony with nature*, Taschen 1997

Vallès-Bled, Maïthé, *Picassiette Visitor's Guide*, The Friends of Chartres Museum 2002

van Zuylen, Gabrielle and de Brissac, Gilles, *Apremont: A French Folly*, Thames and Hudson 1999

Wade, Judith, *Italian Gardens*, Rizzoli 2002

Walter, Marc and Coignard, Jérome, *Dream Palaces*, Vendome Press 2004

Whitelaw, Jeffery W., *Follies*, Shire Publications 2005

Wiseman, Carter, *The Architecture of I.M. Pei*, Thames and Hudson 1990

Zerbst, Rainer, *Antoni Gaudí*, Taschen 1997

www.portmeirion-village.com
www.chateaudegroussay.com

Foremost, I should like to thank Linda Wade, who gave herself unconditionally to make this the book that it is. After eleven other publications, this is the first time that I have been so much a part of the layout and the photographic editing process and, undoubtedly, this is the book of which I am by far the most proud.

I have really enjoyed working alongside Tim Knox and Caroline Holmes — both of whom have been kindred folly-philes. Erica Hunningher has been a very diligent editor and has guided me carefully as the book has progressed. Sarah Kane copy-edited and proofread the book with great sensitivity and intelligence.

My friends have also been of great support: my sister, Maat, Laure de Graumont, Miara Martell, Ingrid and Helmut Marsoner, Simon Wedgwood, Shelly-Anne Claircourt. Also the countless number of patient administrators who arranged permissions thus making the book possible, in particular: Fiona Lindsay, Nadia Tarolla, Judith Wade, librarians at the RIBA Library, London. My special thanks to the Antique Collectors' Club, especially Richard Weale and Stephen Mackinlay.

Last, but not least, the private owners and institutions that permitted me to take photographs of their follies, without which this book would not have been possible.

Nic Barlow
London, 2008

This book was conceived by Barlow & Wade
Edited and designed for Garden Art Press by
Linda Wade Design, 18 Nevern Square, London SW5 9PD

First published in 2008 by Garden Art Press, an imprint of
the Antique Collectors' Club Ltd, Sandy Lane,
Old Martlesham, Woodbridge, Suffolk IP12 4SD

Photographs copyright © Nic Barlow 2008
Text copyright © Caroline Holmes 2008
Introduction copyright © Tim Knox 2008
Editorial, design and layout copyright © Linda Wade Design 2008

The right of Nic Barlow, Caroline Holmes and Tim Knox as the authors of this work has been asserted by them in accordance with the Copyright, Design and Patents Act 1988

A CIP catalogue record for this book is available from the British Library

ISBN 978-1-870673-56-3

Edited by Erica Hunningher
Copy-edited and proofread by Sarah Kane
Index by Richard Bird

Printed in Singapore for the Garden Art Press,
a division of the Antique Collectors' Club Ltd.
Woodbridge, Suffolk IP12 4SD